State of Vermont

# FOREWORD

IN the bewildering cross currents that have engulfed modern life in rapid changes, it has become increasingly evident to educators and others engaged in character training that an inevitable effect has been a paternalistic tendency to regiment the habits and even the very thoughts of both children and adults. This has forced growing life into restrictive channels by prescribed patterns, so that the constructive efforts of education have been frustrated and qualities of individual initiative and self-reliance have been alarmingly submerged.

Boston University, together with other institutions of higher learning, has recognized the seriousness of the problem. It has given careful study to the means of meeting the situation and, in 1930, decided that an opportunity should be offered to its students and to teachers and social workers of surrounding towns to learn a selected number of creative handicrafts so that they might have this means of stimulating self-expression in the daily lives of children and adults.

The response was immediate and enthusiastic, so that these courses have been regularly included in the educational and social science curriculum. Instruction in the different crafts is given by the teachers of the Fellowcrafters Guild, an institution of acknowledged leadership in this field, which has now been affiliated with Boston University.

Numerous requests, however, have been received for

v

## FOREWORD

craft instruction from persons in distant places and others unable to attend the classes. The publishers have generously agreed to join in this social experiment by publishing a series of inexpensive, elementary books, which will give to people remote from Boston exactly the same step-by-step instruction as is afforded to the class students.

Boston University shares with the publishers the hope that *Branford Handicraft Series* will afford its readers a satisfying means of self-expression through creative work.

HENRY H. MEYER, Ph.D., Th.D.,
*Dean of Boston University*
*School of Social Service.*

## PREFACE

IT is often said that there is no joy equal to that of the ability to create. It was the inspiration derived from her joy in weaving which has led the author to write this book.

Weaving is not a difficult art and the pleasure derived from accomplishment will far outweigh the hours spent in learning the technicalities which must precede efficiency.

*Hand Loom Weaving for Amateurs* attempts to tell you plainly and simply the various steps necessary to a knowledge of the subject. Study it carefully, step by step, and your reward will be an unmeasurable joy in self-expression. In addition you will have the continued pleasure of living with the beautiful things which you yourself have made.

The author takes this opportunity to express her appreciation to Constantine Belash, President of Fellow-crafters, Inc., for his friendly interest in this field, as well as his breadth of vision which has co-ordinated the allied arts and crafts.

A word of appreciation is also due William Penn Newby for his accurate and artistic drawings which have been of incalculable assistance where methods have been difficult to describe; and to W. Forbes Robertson, of The Beacon Press, Inc., and Leslie A. Boswell, whose many valuable suggestions have helped to give this manual its final form.

# TABLE OF CONTENTS

# TABLE OF CONTENTS

# CHAPTER I

## The Romantic Story of Weaving

WEAVING, the interlacing of long strands with shorter cross strands to form a smooth, close, and inseparable surface, extends so far back into the unrecorded dawn of civilization that its beginnings can be only conjectured. History offers no explanation of the origin of the art, for by the time the art of writing had been acquired, weaving was so far advanced that it was an accepted feature of life, needing no special comment.

Archæological investigations, however, have discovered that in whatever center a civilized life was developed, even thousands of years before the birth of Christ, the implements for spinning and hand weaving were also known and in practically the same form, whether among the earliest Egyptians, the Scandinavians of the Bronze Age, the Lake Dwellers, the Aztecs or Peruvians, the wandering peoples of Asia, the hill tribes of India, the natives of Central Africa or the islanders of the Pacific.

The earliest weaving was done with grasses and herbs or whatever was found long enough for the purpose. In fact, old looms of the West Indies for weaving grasses show a shuttle and a batten to beat the weft upward and compress it into the warp. An improvement of undatable origin is shown in an Indian hill-tribesman's loom, which had rudely constructed heddles for raising and lowering the rows of the warp threads, as the shuttle

1

carried the weft threads across. A hanging comb was pulled forward to press the warp and the weft together.

The special development of spinning and weaving in different centers of civilization was inevitably determined by the natural resources available. In Egypt, flax was used at a very early date. Egyptian mummies, shrouded with linen coverings of very finely spun thread, closely woven, show the marvelous skill of these early weavers. Paintings of weavers at work, both on vertical and horizontal looms, adorn the tombs of Beni Hasson of Egypt, 2800–2600 B.C.

In China, the spinning and weaving of silk started about 3000 B.C., though the weaving of other materials may have been practiced before this date. According to Chinese historians, the discovery of the art of reeling and spinning silk was accredited to Se Ling She, the wife of the third emperor of China, about 2640 B.C., and she was thereafter known as the "Goddess of the Silkworm." For many years silk weaving was confined exclusively to China. Silk was sold in Greece and Syria for its weight in gold. So jealously did the Chinese guard the industry that a death penalty was imposed on anyone who should reveal the art to an outsider. But in 550 A.D., two monks, by the order of the Roman emperor, Justinian, smuggled a supply of silkworm eggs in hollow bamboo staffs and carried them to Constantinople. By that time, however, the knowledge of silk weaving had spread from southern Asia into Japan, Persia, India, and Egypt and there to the Coptic weavers, who had already gained a reputation for their skill with wool and flax. In the year 30 B.C., when the Romans conquered Egypt, the Coptic weavers, as slaves, wove the silk and woolen materials used by their Roman overlords.

Large herds of native sheep in Assyria, Babylonia, and Persia led to the development of wool weaving in these countries. The wool was made into rugs of marvelous softness and beauty, with the ideas for color and the colors themselves furnished by natural berries and leaves. This industry of hand woven rugs, which began thousands of years ago, still endures, undiminished and unsurpassed.

These centers have been mentioned because of their early prominence but, as has been stated, the art of weaving one material or another was developed in every country inhabited by civilized man. Old Greek vases, for instance, have pictures of looms described as belonging to Penelope and Circe, characters of ancient Greek mythology.

As a result of trade and conquest, the art of the early weavers of the Orient spread beyond the shores of the Mediterranean. New centers grew in Algeria, Malaga, Granada, and Seville, which became celebrated for their patterned silks and stuffs long before the Christian conquest.

On the Island of Sicily, which for many centuries had been a prominent trading post, Saracenic weavers had long been established. In 1147 A.D., Robert of Sicily invaded Greece and conquered the cities of Athens, Thebes, and Corinth, then a part of the Byzantine Empire, and captured a number of Byzantine weavers whom he settled in Palermo. Thus the Saracenic and the Byzantine styles of weaving intermingled. Soon the cities of Sicily and, in the following century, those of Italy, notably, Lucca, Florence, Milan, Genoa, and Venice, became important centers of silk manufacture.

Not many years later, the Saracenic and the Byzantine

weavers, fleeing from Lucca and Florence, wandered to
the north and the east and carried their art to Germany
and France, where Lyons especially became noted. In
the countries through which these weavers had passed,
hand woven silks of exquisite beauty were produced in
the various monasteries during the latter half of the
Middle Ages.

In Britain, the early inhabitants may have had a knowledge of some kind of weaving before the Roman conquest of the island in 43 B.C., though there are no records
to prove it. At that time, however, wool weaving was
definitely introduced and continued to be practiced by
the natives.   In 1066, when William I invaded England,
he took with him Flemish weavers, who, after the conquest, settled in the country and started the making of
homespun cloth. This is still an important industry of
England and Ireland. Farther to the north, weavers in
Scotland developed and, to this day, excel in the weaving
of plaids and other woolen cloth of finely hand spun
yarn unequaled for its durability.

Yet with all the development of the different weaving
centers and the assembled and the intermingled skill of
different nationalities, the original hand loom remained
practically unchanged.

In 1533, a foot treadle had been added to the spinning
wheel. In the year 1800, however, a French mechanic,
Joseph Jacquard, applied his genius to the invention of
a mechanically operated loom which still bears his name.
By the use of perforated cards, he worked out various
intricate patterns for brocades. Since Jacquard's time, in-
numerable inventions and improvements have been added
until the great looms of modern industry have been
developed, which, with their complex machinery, can

produce an infinite variety of materials. The mechanical looms, however, have not been able to surpass or even equal the softness, the charm, and the durability of the fabrics made by skilled hand weavers, or the masterpieces of the weaving art from early China, India, and Persia, which, carefully treasured and preserved in various art museums, offer the chief source of inspiration and suggestion to the hand weaver of today.

# CHAPTER II

## EASIWEAVE

ONE of the simplest methods of weaving is that in which a blunt needle is used to carry a thread under every other *warp* (lengthwise threads), as in darning.

In all weaving there are five steps to be considered:

1. The article, its use, and the materials best adapted to that use.
2. Color and design must be studied in connection with materials used.
3. Warp and warping of loom.
4. A method of separating the warp threads, to allow the weft threads to be passed through.
5. A device for beating the weft threads together.

In connection with the first two steps, the value of visits to the textile departments and the Chinese, Japanese, and Persian rooms in near-by museums cannot be too strongly stressed, for by this study you will be able to establish a sense of values which will save hours of experimentation in the school or studio.

Texture of the material also comes under this heading. A material for a bag to be carried with a coat or a winter suit might be of a rough texture, while a small bag to be carried with a dress to a tea or a bridge party should be of soft silk or wool in colors to harmonize, or as an article of contrast to the other costume accessories. Wall hangings, runners, ties, luncheon sets, chenille face cloths, and scarfs, each demands an understanding of the material best fitted for the purpose.

The third step, warp and warping, is the first fundamental step in weaving, the first two steps being more in the form of preparation. *Warp* and *weft* are the first terms with which the beginner becomes familiar. The warp are the threads which run lengthwise of the loom or frame. The weft, or woof, threads are those woven across the warp to form the web or woven material.

Under the fourth step, in the separating of the warp threads to allow the weft threads to be passed through, a long blunt needle may be used to carry a thread under every other warp, as in darning, or a heddle rod (See Glossary) having every other warp thread tied to it with loops, may be used to open a real shed (See Glossary) to pass the shuttle through.

Under the fifth heading, a device for beating the weft threads together—a forked stick was used by the American Indians; a table fork or a comb is used by tapestry weavers today.

## The Easiweave Frame

The Easiweave frame, or loom, is a square, hard wood frame (which may also be made in the form of an oblong), with grooved edges. By these grooves, a looped edge, the same length as the width of the frame, is formed on the woven material. Through the grooves, yarn is wound horizontally and vertically; needle weaving binds the windings of the yarn together.

Easiweave frames, or looms, come in a number of sizes. The small five-inch frame makes a square of which the center woven part is three and one-half inches, with half-inch loops on the outside. These squares may be made of cotton or rope linen, for tumbler or finger bowl doilies, or of wool, for children's bags for change or marbles. The wool squares may be crocheted together and made into larger bags and, with a lining, are ideal for knitting bags. A light, warm afghan may be made in a similar manner by crocheting the loops of the small wool square together. About twelve yards of Germantown or Tapestry wool are required to make a four and one-half inch square. A frame, seven and one-half inches by nine and one-half inches, is the size used for a zipper purse, which may be made in a plaid or striped design, while on the eleven by fourteen-inch frame, may be made attractive raffia plate mats for the breakfast service on the terrace in summer. A frame, five and one-half inches by twenty-three inches, is the size used for knitted suit belts, neckties, and long narrow runners.

## PLAIN WEAVE

EQUIPMENT:

    Easiweave Frame, 5″

    Needle, 6″

    Germantown or Tapestry wool

    A 12½ yd. skein, Tapestry wool will make one plain color square; though two colors are usually used, as this gives a more interesting effect.

PROCESS:

Place the small Easiweave frame on the table with corner A at the weaver's right (Plate I). Begin by fastening the yarn, passing it two or three times around the lower frame at the first groove at the right, leaving three

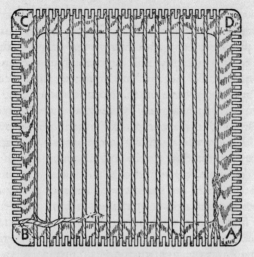

PLATE I

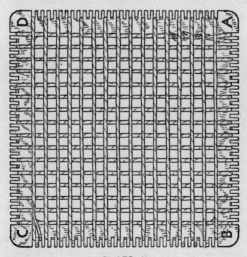

PLATE II

inches of the yarn to be later securely fastened. Wind the yarn on the frame by carrying it over the front of the frame to the top and through the first groove. The yarn is next passed around the back, skipping one groove, and brought through the third groove and down to a corresponding groove on the lower front of the frame. This winding process of skipping every other groove continues in this manner, working from the right to the left side of the frame, ending in the lower left corner.

Turn the frame so that corner B is now at the right. (See Plate II.)

Pass the yarn underneath at corner B and bring it through the first groove at the lower front of the frame to the first groove on the upper front of the frame. The yarn is now carried by skipping every other groove, working from the right to the left on the frame, ending at lower left corner C. A three-inch length of yarn is again left at this corner to be fastened securely into the weaving.

We now have two ends of the yarn, that which was temporarily fastened at the beginning of our weaving and that which is finished at this point. These ends are each to be permanently fastened, as shown in Plate V, Figure A.

Turn the frame so that corner C is at the lower right. (See Plate III.)

The second color is now used, allowing a three-inch end and starting at the lower front of the frame, corner C, second groove. The winding process of skipping every other groove continues as before and ends in the next to the last groove on the under side of the upper left frame.

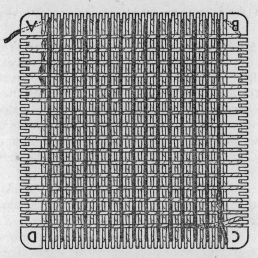

PLATE III

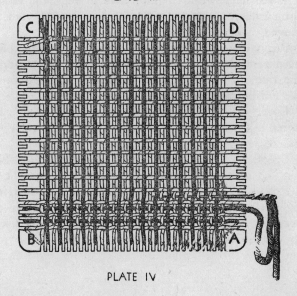

PLATE IV

Turn the frame again, having corner A at the right. (See Plate IV.)

The yarn is passed under the corner and brought out through the second groove at the right edge. Measure off a four-yard length of yarn to be used in the needle weaving. Start by going under the first vertical thread, over the second vertical thread, and under the third, continuing to weave by alternating through to the left side. The yarn is then passed around the back of the third groove, coming up to the front of the frame through groove four, and is to be woven under and over the vertical threads from the left to the right. This step of weaving is finished at the upper left side of the frame, corner C. Pass the thread through the upper groove on the left side of the frame, diagonally under corner C, and through the first groove, corner C, upper frame. The remaining yarn length is used to hemstitch around the outside edge of the square before the loops are removed, as shown in Plate V, Figure B.

Remove the weaving from the frame using a blunt needle and starting from the center of the under side of the frame. This method prevents uneven stretching of the finished square.

Cover with a damp cloth before pressing with a hot iron.

### BASKET WEAVE
#### (See Plate V, Figure D)

Place the frame with corner A, as in Plate I, at the right. Leave a three-inch end for finishing. Carry the yarn to the first groove, upper right, across the back to the second upper groove bringing it through to the front and down to the second groove from the right on the

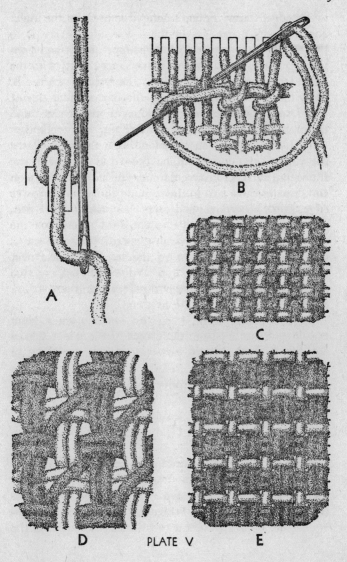

A

B

C

D          PLATE V          E

lower edge. Carry the yarn across the back on the lower edge, skip two grooves in the lower edge, carry it to the corresponding groove in the upper edge, and continue in this way across the frame from the right to the left, ending on the under side of the frame at corner B. Now bring the yarn diagonally across the under side of the frame, through to the front of the frame, and through the first groove at the left side of corner B.

Turn the frame so that corner B is at the right. Carry the yarn to the corresponding groove in the top of the frame and through groove number one and back through and down groove two to the second groove on the lower edge, skip two grooves and carry it up through the fifth groove on the lower edge to the fifth groove on the upper edge, and down through the sixth. Continue across the frame from the right to the left, using the next groove each time on the upper edge and skipping two on the lower edge. Leave a three-inch end and fasten at corner C, also fasten the first end.

Take the second color. Turn the frame so corner C is at the right. Start at corner C; leave a three-inch end, take the yarn through the first groove in the lower right edge and bring it up to and through the first groove on the upper edge; skip the two grooves already filled in and bring it down through the fourth on the upper edge to the fourth on the lower edge; up through the fifth groove to the fifth groove at the top. Continue this process and finish at corner A.

Place the frame in the original position with corner A at the right. Carry the wool underneath diagonally across corner A to the third groove at the right edge. Measure three and one-half yards of this color and thread the weaving needle. Weave under the first outside threads, over the

second two, under the third two, continue to corner B
over the last single thread; down through the third
groove on the left edge, up through the fourth groove,
and weave back beside your first row to the right edge;
down through the fourth groove on the right edge and
up through the seventh groove. Continue this process
to the top of the frame. Leave the end for final finish of
hemstitching around the outside edge of the now woven
square.

For hemstitching and removal from the frame, see
page 12.

A further variation may be made in this pattern by
using a diagonal weave of the first color. (Plate V,
Figure D.) To add this additional variation, place the
frame in the first position with corner A at the right.

Begin at corner A, leave a three-inch end in the sixth
groove from the bottom at the right. Carry the needle
diagonally underneath, first crossing at corner A, down
through the sixth groove from the right edge at the
bottom, up through the tenth groove at the bottom,
under the dark crosses, (Plate V, Figure D), over the
light crosses, down through the tenth groove on the
right side, up through the fourteenth groove on the
right, across the loom diagonally, down through the
fourteenth groove on the lower edge, and so on. The
diagonal crossing one way will take about two and one-
half yards of yarn.


## ALTERNATING WEAVE

*(See Plate V, Figure E)*

Place the frame with corner A at the right. Leave a
three-inch end of yarn for finishing and begin at corner

A by carrying the yarn up to the first groove at the top. Pass the yarn in back and bring it down through the second groove at the top to the corresponding groove at the lower edge. Skip a groove in the lower edge each time around, but each time bring yarn down through the next groove at the top. Finish this process at corner C.

Place corner B at the right; pass the yarn underneath diagonally at corner C and up through the groove and over to the corresponding groove at the top. Carry the yarn around through the next groove and down to the corresponding groove at the bottom. Skip a groove and carry the yarn up to the top of the frame through groove four. Pass in back through and down the next groove—finishing at corner A. Fasten the ends. Place the frame in the first position with corner A at the right and, with the second color, fill in the single grooves ending at corner B.

Place the frame with corner B at the right, and measure three and one-half yards of the second color, and weave under the first vertical thread and over the second; under the next two, and so on, across the frame.

For the hemstitching and the removal of the weaving from the frame, see page 12.

## Easiweave Zipper Purse, 5½″ × 6½″

EQUIPMENT:

  Easiweave Frame, 7½ ″ × 9½ ″
  1 Needle, 2″, Tapestry
  1 Needle, 5″, with curved point
  2 Skeins—36 yds. Tapestry wool or the same amount of Germantown.

1 Skein—12½ yds. harmonizing color (green-blue and
     a light value henna, or tan and a middle value
     henna are both pleasing combinations.)

1 Zipper—5½"

Lining—Silk 11" × 19"

For the weave, see Plate V, Figure C. An attractive
pattern may be obtained by running a different tone of
the same color, or a contrasting color, across the bag
from the left to the right, thus creating a striped effect.


PROCESS:

Place the frame on the table with the greater length
of the frame running from the right to the left. Mark
the upper right corner of the frame "A," the upper
left corner of the frame "B." Begin at the first upper
right groove, at corner A, carry yarn down across the
back to the first groove from the right on the lower
edge, and completely around to the first groove of the
upper edge, across the back to the third groove on the
upper edge, and down the front to the third groove on
the lower edge, across the front, skipping the fourth
groove, down the back, through the fifth groove on the
lower edge, up and through the fifth groove on the
upper edge. Continue this process of winding the yarn
on the frame, finishing at corner B. This will close the
lower edge for the bottom of the bag and leave the top
to be slipped off the frame when finished.

Cut a piece of paper or cardboard of such dimensions
that it can be placed flat on the upper side of the frame.
Slip it underneath the front warp threads to prevent the
catching of the threads when needle weaving.

Carry the yarn diagonally across the front of corner B
and through the upper left groove, and across the back

to the first upper right groove. Bring it through to the front of the right side, skip a groove and return to the back through the third groove. Carry the yarn across the back from the third groove at the right, to the third groove at the left. Bring the yarn through groove three, skip a groove and carry it through groove five, across the back, to groove five at the right. Continue this process to the bottom of the frame, finishing at the front.

This process of winding on the back of the frame must now be repeated on the front. Place the frame in the original position, with corner A at the right. Begin by placing the yarn through the second upper right groove, continue down the back to the second lower right groove, and carry the yarn through the second right groove on the lower edge to the front, then completely around to the upper edge, and through the second upper right groove to the back. Skip a groove and bring it up through the fourth groove. Continue this winding process by filling in the unused grooves, finishing at corner B.

The needle weaving now begins at the upper edge, working from the right to the left, under the first thread, over the second, under the third, over the fourth, and so on, finishing at the left by carrying the yarn through the second upper left groove, around the back, skipping one groove and bringing it through to the front, through the fourth left groove, weaving across the front, and so on, to the last groove. From this point on, the needle weaving is done by weaving back and forth, being careful not to draw in the edges, weaving seven rows on the front and six rows on the back.

The outside edges of both sides of the bag are bound by the hemstitching process shown in Plate V, Figure B.

To remove the bag from the frame, start at the upper

center of the frame and, with a blunt needle, remove the loops, first from the front and then from the back, until all loops at the top have been released. Then remove the loops from each side beginning at the center.

*Making up:*

Press with a hot iron, using a damp cloth. Turn in the loops on the edges, using a running stitch, so they will be caught to the fabric for three-eighths of an inch. Care should be taken not to let the stitches show on the outside. With soft, loosely woven material it is best to run the edge twice.

Measure the lining. For an inside pocket allow six inches more than is required for the bag. A three-inch tuck, stitched at the top with two rows of stitching running down the center, forms the pocket. Stitch the lining to the zipper on each side. Then backstitch the side edges of the lining.

Match the bag at the side, fold it inside out and sew the edges with an overhand stitch. Turn the bag right side out, slip in the lining, and hem the bag to the zipper edge.

## Easiweave Plate Mat

The largest Easiweave frame may be used in making linen or mercerized cotton plate mats. Tumbler mats to match are made on the small frames. This type of weave is illustrated in Plate V, Figure E.

EQUIPMENT:
    Easiweave Frame, 11″ × 14″
    1 Needle, 5″, with curved point

MATERIALS:

    90 yds. of the background color of either rope linen or mercerized cotton.

    10 yds. of contrasting color to be used for the border.

    In this project a background of white and a border of blue is used. The finished mat will have a fringe extending from the inside edge of the frame to the outside, therefore whenever a change of color necessitates the knotting together of the threads, the knots must be made at the extreme outside edge of the frame in order not to appear in the fringe.

PROCESS:

In using linen or mercerized cotton which does not stretch, it is necessary to leave the thread loose. This slack will be taken up in the weaving.

Place the frame on the table with the short edge running from right to left. Letter the lower right corner "A" and the lower left corner "B." Begin the first process at corner A, right edge. Tie a knot in the end of the white thread.

Place the knot at the back of the first lower right groove at corner A, carry the thread up to the first groove at the top. Pass in back, skip a groove, then bring down across the front to the corresponding groove on the lower edge, skip a groove on both the lower and the upper edge each time around. Finish this process at the upper left corner.

Place corner B at the right. Pass the thread underneath diagonally at the left corner and through the first left groove on the lower edge and up through the corresponding groove on the upper edge, pass in back, skipping one groove, bring down through the third groove on the upper edge to the corresponding groove on the lower edge, skip one groove on the lower edge and then up through the corresponding groove on the upper edge. This gives three white threads. Continue this process of skipping every other groove, using six blue threads for the left-end border, twenty-seven white threads for center, six blue threads for the right-end border, three rows of white threads, and finish at corner A.

Place the frame with corner A at the right. Fill in the single grooves with white threads, beginning at corner A. When corner B is reached, pass the thread through the second lower groove, then underneath, and up through the first groove to the second groove, upper frame, and follow the winding back to corner A. There should now be a double thread in every other groove from B to A.

Thread the five-inch needle with one yard of white for the first three rows of weaving. Begin at the right, weaving under the first vertical thread, over the second two, under the next, and so on, across the frame. After weaving three rows of white, join the blue at the edge of the frame, so that the knot will not appear in the fringe, and weave five rows for the first border; weave twenty-eight rows of white for the center; then five rows of blue for the second border, three rows of white, and needle weave back to corner A. Reverse this last process, weaving a second thread parallel and in the same grooves. Hemstitch the outside edge, as shown in Plate V, Figure B. Remove it from the frame and cut the fringe so the ends are even.

## Easiweave Tumbler Mat

Tumbler mats are one of the smaller projects which can be made on the Easiweave frame. The type of weave used is illustrated in Plate V, Figure E.

EQUIPMENT:
Easiweave Frame, 5"
1 Needle, 6"

MATERIALS:
25 yds. of the background color. Use either rope linen or mercerized cotton.
5 yds. of the contrasting color for the border.
In this project the white with the blue as a contrasting color will match the plate mat described above.

PROCESS:
Fringe will be used for the edge, therefore in changing colors, knots must be tied at the extreme outside edge of the frame, in order not to appear in the fringe.

It is necessary to leave the thread loose, in winding either linen or cotton on the frame, as they do not stretch. This slack will be taken up in the weaving.

Place the frame with corner A at the right (Plate I). Tie a knot on the end of the white thread. Place the knot at the back of the first lower right groove at corner A, carry the thread up to the first groove at the top. Pass the thread in the back and skip a groove, bring it down across the front to the corresponding groove on the lower edge; knot the blue at the back of the frame, for the right border, skip a groove on the lower edge, carry it up to the corresponding groove on the upper edge, skip a groove and bring it down to the corresponding groove on the lower edge; knot the white thread at the back of the lower edge. Continue this process of skipping every other groove on the lower and the upper edges until there are eight white threads for the center, two blue threads for the left border, and two white threads; end at corner C.

Turn the frame with corner B at the right, pass the white thread underneath diagonally at corner B, and then through the first right groove on the lower edge and up through the corresponding groove on the upper edge, pass it in back, skip one groove, bring it down through the third groove on the upper edge to the corresponding groove on the lower edge, continue this process of skipping every other groove, using two blue threads for the border, eight white threads for the center, two blue threads for the border, and two white threads for the left edge.

Turn the frame with corner C at the right. Bring the white thread diagonally across the back of corner C to the second groove on the lower right edge up to the corresponding groove at the top, knot the blue thread at the back of the frame and continue filling in the unused grooves on the lower edge and the upper edge, using three blue threads for the border, seven white threads for the center, three blue threads for the border, and one white thread at the left edge. When corner A is reached, carry the thread through the second groove on the upper edge and underneath and up through the first groove. Follow this last winding back to corner C, using the same colors for the corresponding rows. There should now be a double thread in every other groove from corner C to corner D.

Thread the six-inch needle with nine inches of white thread, carry the white thread underneath corner C diagonally and up through the second groove on the right edge. Begin needle weaving under one, over two, under one, over two, and so on, to the left edge. Continue needle weaving, tying a knot at the back of the frame for each change of color. Twelve inches of blue for the two rows of the border; one and one-quarter yards of white for the seven rows of the center; twelve inches of blue for the two rows of the border, and nine inches of white for the last row of white. In order to have two parallel threads to complete the weave, carry the thread down the second groove on the upper edge and up through the first groove, following the needle weaving back to corner C. This will complete the double thread weaving. Hemstitch around the outside edge, as shown in Plate V, Figure B. Remove the weaving from the frame.

### Raffia Plate Mat and Tumbler Mat

Raffia has many interesting and attractive uses. It is, however, more difficult to handle than many of the other weaving materials, and it is therefore suggested that the beginner use some of the easier materials before attempting its use.

EQUIPMENT:
>     Easiweave Frame, 11″ × 14″
>     Easiweave Frame, 5″ square
>     1 Needle, 3″ Tapestry
>     2 Needles, 6″ and 5″ with curved point

MATERIALS:
>     1 half-pound Hank of Gray Raffia
>     1    "      "      "    " Peach Raffia
>     (This amount will make about six Plate Mats.)

The type of weave used is illustrated in Plate V, Figure E.

PROCESS:

Since raffia comes in short lengths it will be necessary to plan that the knots, which join the strands, are so tied that they will not appear in either the woven mat or on the outside edges of the mat, which will serve as a fringe.

Place the frame on the table with the short edge running from the right to the left, letter the lower right corner "A" and the lower left corner "B." Prepare the raffia for use by removing the hard roll on either edge, leaving a strip about three-eighths or one-half an inch wide. Begin with a strand of the color you wish to have predominate in the mat, tie a knot in the smaller end of the strand and follow the same process used in making plate mats of mercerized cotton or linen. (See page 19.)

### Worsted Bag With Cut-Out Wooden Handles

An attractive pattern can be obtained by using a harmonizing or a contrasting color in stripes running across the bag from the right to the left. These stripes are introduced in the winding of the second group of threads and the needle weaving. For the bag shown in Plate VI, a brown was used for the principal color, with dark brown, orange, and yellow for the contrast.

EQUIPMENT:

    Easiweave Frame, 11″ × 14″
    1 Needle, 3″ Tapestry
    1 Needle with Curved Point, 5″

MATERIALS:

    4 skeins Tapestry Wool, 36 yds. each, or the same amount of Germantown.

3 skeins, 12 yds. each, of harmonizing or contrasting
colors for borders.

Lining—silk, 12" × 32"

Handles, 1 pr., 2½" × 9¼"

PLATE VI

PROCESS:

Place the frame on the table with the greater length
running from the right to the left. Mark the upper right
corner "A," and the upper left corner "B." Begin at the
first upper groove, corner A, leaving a three-inch end
for fastening. (See Plate V, Figure A.) Carry the yarn
down across the back to the corresponding groove on

the lower edge, through and up the front to the first right groove on the upper edge, through and down the front to the third groove on the lower edge, through to the back and up to the third groove on the upper edge, through to the front skipping the fourth groove, through the fifth groove to the back and down, continuing around to the fifth groove, upper edge. Continue this process of winding the yarn on the frame, and finish by bringing the yarn up across the front to the last upper left groove at corner B. This will close the lower edge for the bottom of the bag and allow the top to be slipped off when finished.

Carry the yarn underneath diagonally across corner B and up through the upper left groove. Carry the yarn from the left to the right across the front of the frame to the upper right groove, through to the back, skip a groove, up through the third groove on the right edge. Carry the yarn across the front to the third groove on the left side, through to the back, skip a groove and return to the front. Continue this process until there are fourteen horizontal rows of brown. Take the dark brown yarn, tie it at the edge of the frame to the brown yarn and continue for two rows, in the same manner, then tie; and wind four rows of yellow yarn, one row of dark brown yarn, five rows of orange yarn, one row of dark brown yarn, four rows of yellow yarn, and two rows of dark brown yarn. As this brings the winding to the end of the side grooves, fasten the end of the dark brown yarn.

Turn the frame over so that corner A is at the left underside of the frame. Cut a piece of heavy paper or cardboard of such dimensions that it can be placed on the upper side of the frame underneath the warp threads, which will prevent any catching of the yarn when needle weaving.

Repeat the process of winding the horizontal threads on the second side, as described above.

Place the frame in the original position with corner A at the right. Place the yarn in the second upper right groove, carry it down the back to the second lower right groove, continue around to the second upper groove, carry the yarn to the back, skip a groove and bring it up through the fourth groove, continue this process, filling in unused grooves, finishing at corner B.

The needle weaving now begins with the brown yarn at the first upper unused groove at corner A, and weaving from the right to the left, under the first vertical thread, over the second, under the third, and so on, to the left edge. Fill in the unused grooves with the colors as follows: fourteen rows of brown yarn, one row of dark brown yarn, four rows of yellow yarn, one row of dark brown yarn, six rows of orange yarn, one row of dark brown yarn, four rows of yellow yarn, and one row of dark brown yarn. The next eight rows are of the brown yarn; begin these by weaving under the first right vertical thread, over the second, under the third, and so on, across the frame, ending under the first left vertical thread; carry the yarn over the first left vertical thread, under the second left vertical thread, and so on; repeat this weaving for eight rows, being careful not to draw in the edges.

The needle weaving on the second side is the same, except that nine rows of brown yarn are used at the bottom. This allows one thread for the bottom edge or middle of bag. Fasten the outside edges by hemstitching (Plate V, Figure B).

To remove the bag from the frame, start at the upper center of the frame and, with a small blunt needle, remove the loops first from the front, then from the back, until all the loops at the top have been released. Start at the center of each side and release all the loops.

*Making up:*

Place a damp cloth over the bag and press it with a hot iron. Turn in all the loose edges on the wrong side and sew them down so they will be firmly caught to the fabric, being careful not to let the stitches show on the outside. With loosely woven material it is best to run the edges twice.

Match the stripes at the sides of the bag, and with an overhand stitch sew the sides to within three inches of the top. Turn the bag right side out, and press.

Turn in one-half inch on one of the short sides of the lining. Determine the length of the lining by measuring from the turned-in edge to the bottom of the bag. Allow a six-inch tuck if a pocket is desired. For a pocket-lining, twelve by twenty-inch silk is required. Stitch the top of the tuck and have two rows of stitching down the center. Backstitch the sides of the lining and make the lining slightly smaller than the outside of the bag. Then slip in the lining and hem to the upper edges of the bag.

Wooden handles can be made of gumwood, walnut, or mahogany, three-sixteenths of an inch thick. Those illustrated in Plate VI are of gumwood which has a pleasing grain of many tones of brown.

Gather in the side of the bag to fit the handle, allowing about an inch for fullness which will give the bag a more attractive appearance than if the handle is sewed to the bag without this allowance.

# CHAPTER III

## THE EASIWEAVE ADJUSTABLE FRAME

### (*See Plate VII*)

EASIWEAVE ADJUSTABLE FRAMES of durable, hard wood come in sections six inches long, each containing thirty-three pins. These sections, joined by brass bolts, form any size frame desired.

Four sections may be used for making the small squares which, when woven, measure four and three-quarter inches square. These squares may be put together to make attractive bags, hats, sweaters, coats, afghans, doilies, table covers, bedspreads, and table-cloths. Six pieces joined together form a piece of material four and three-quarters inches by ten inches. Three pieces joined together form one side of a knitting bag, nine and one-half inches by fourteen and one-half inches, which can be attached to wooden handles.

The Easiweave Adjustable Frame forms an edge of one thread, interlaced with those on either side of it, by the use of pins instead of grooves to hold the yarn, as in the Easiweave.

EQUIPMENT:
> Frame, six sections
> 1 Needle, 6″

MATERIALS:
> 1 skein, 36 yds. Tapestry yarn
> 1 skein, 12 yds. Tapestry yarn

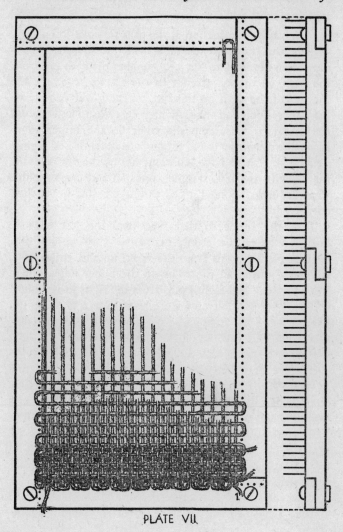

PLATE VII.

PROCESS:

Join frame, one section wide, two sections long.

Place the frame on the table with the short side running from the right to the left. Number the fifth pin from the right on the lower edge of the frame, "No. 1." Tie the end of the yarn on this pin, on the lower edge leaving a three-inch end for fastening, carry it up and around the first two pins from the right on the upper edge. Bring the yarn down and around the seventh and eighth pins on the lower edge, continue across the frame from the right to the left, skipping one pin and carrying the yarn around the next two, ending at the lower left corner.

Turn the frame so that what was the left edge is horizontally in the front, carry the yarn around the fourth and fifth pins from the right, up and around the first two pins from the right on the upper edge, down to the seventh and eighth pins from the right lower edge, continue across the frame from right to left, and end by going around the fifth and sixth pins on the upper edge and around the first pin on the upper left edge.

Place the frame with the first section marked No. 1 at the top. Carry the yarn up from the first pin on the lower left edge and around the sixth and seventh pins from the left on the upper edge; bring it down and around the third and fourth pins from the left lower edge, continue across the frame from the left to the right, skipping one pin, and carrying the yarn around the next two, ending at the upper right corner; leave a three-inch end for fastening.

Place the frame in its original position.

Take a needle with seven yards of the second color;

begin at the lower right edge between the row of pins at the bottom and the first pin on the right edge; run the needle under the first vertical thread, over the second, under the third, and continue across the frame from the right to the left, ending under the last outside thread; around the fifth and sixth pins on the left edge and across the frame from the left to the right under the first vertical thread, over the second and continue back and forth across the frame from the right to the left and reverse, ending at the upper right corner. Take this end and pass it around the fifth pin from the top on the right edge and back, into the same strand. Finish the remaining three ends as shown in Plate V, Figure A, and remove from the frame as described on page 12.

# CHAPTER IV

## FELLOWCRAFTERS SCHOOL LOOMS

### (*See Plate VIII*)

THIS is a flat loom of the Indian type, which has cord heddles attached to heddle rods for opening a shed through which to pass the shuttle.

### CHENILLE FACE CLOTH

As the process of warping the Fellowcrafters School Loom is practically the same for each type of article woven, it is suggested that one first warp the frame for the making of a chenille face cloth.

EQUIPMENT:
    Fellowcrafters School Loom
    Heddle Rods
    3 Shuttles
    Board for making heddles
    "C" clamp
    A Fork or Forked Stick

MATERIALS:
    Natural colored carpet warp
    Rose      "     "     "
    White Cotton Chenille, 1 skein, small
    Rose      "     " for border, 10 yds.

PROCESS:
  In making any article on the Fellowcrafters School Loom, two colors will be used for the warp and it is

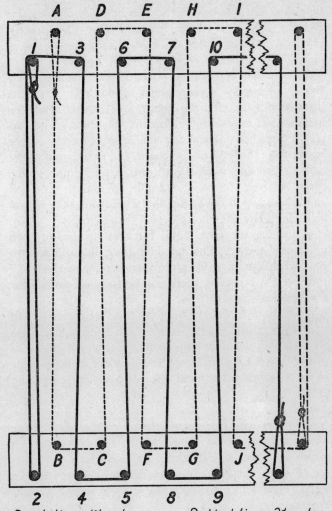

Dark line, 1st color.          Dotted line, 2d color.

PLATE VIII

suggested that one-half the heddles be made of one color and the other half of the second color. This process, using the heddles of two colors, will assist the weaver in clearly distinguishing each shed when weaving.

For the heddles, take a board about two inches by twelve inches by seven-eighths of an inch, or more, drive two nails into the board, one at each end, ten inches apart as shown in Plate IX, Figure A. Then attach a thread to one nail and wind the thread around the nail at the other end of the board, and return to the first nail by crossing over the thread in the center of the space between the nails, continue around the first nail and cross again in the center and wind around the second nail. (See Plate IX, Figure B.)

In making the face cloth, forty-six heddles of each color are needed. The winding must be sufficient so that when cut in half at the intersection, marked "X" on Plate IX, Figure B, there will be forty-six threads for the heddles.

After the threads have been cut they are carefully tied with an overhand knot (See Plate IX, Figures C and D) which makes the large loop or heddle around each thread of the warp of similar length and they are then put aside to be later passed around the warp of corresponding color.

*Warping:* The first set of the warp threads is made with a natural colored carpet warp (See Plate VIII) in which the warp is represented by numbers. The second set of warp threads is made with rose colored carpet warp (Plate VIII) in which the warp is represented by letters.

The warping is completed after forty-six threads of

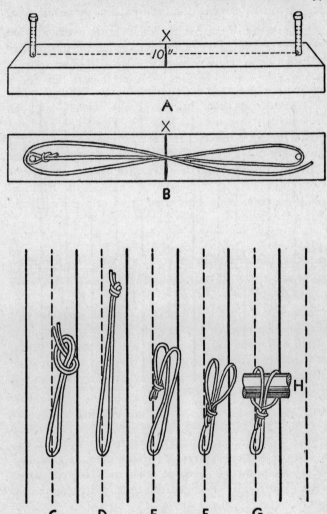

PLATE IX

each color have been warped. There will be an extra outside thread of the natural and an extra outside thread of the rose colored warp. The illustration for this process is shown on the extreme right in Plate VIII. This actually makes forty-seven threads of each color, but for a

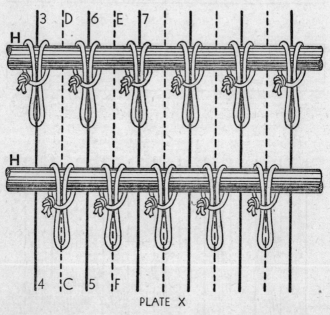

PLATE X

working purpose each of the outside double edges is considered and used as one.

The heddles are next attached to the warp threads of a corresponding color. Then the heddles are looped over the heddle rod as shown in Plate IX, Figures E, F, and G.

After both sets of heddles are attached, a proper shed is made by alternating—lifting first one, then the other, heddle rod. Plate X shows the heddles properly attached. Plate XI shows a shuttle in the process of being passed from the right to the left between the two sets of warp threads.

*Weaving:* Wind one shuttle with the natural colored warp, one with white chenille, and the other with rose chenille. Use a "C" clamp and fasten the loom to the desk or table.

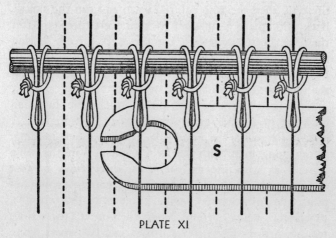

PLATE XI

Take the shuttle of the natural colored warp, raise the heddle rod, pull the natural colored warp threads up with the left hand and, with the right hand, run the shuttle from the right to the left through the shed thus formed. Leave three inches of this weft thread at the right end. (See Plate XII, Figure A.) To fasten, carry it around the double end thread at the right side of the loom (Plate XII, Figure B) tucking it for one-half inch in the same row as the second weft thread.

Raise the heddle rod, pull up the rose warp threads

with the right hand and run the shuttle through the shed
thus formed, from the left to the right, leaving the
thread at a slant as shown in Plate XII, Figure C. This
prevents the edges from drawing in. Use a fork or forked
stick for "beating" the thread into place. Begin at the
right (See Plate XII, Figure D) and work across the
loom toward the left (Plate XII, Figure E). Continue
raising first the natural colored warp and run the shuttle
through, then the rose colored warp and run the shuttle
back until there is one-half inch of weft threads. After
they are beaten together, cut the weft thread, leaving
three inches at the end. Fasten as shown in Plate XII,
Figure A, remembering that the end must be tucked in
the same shed as the last row of color.

Now use the shuttle with the white chenille, fastening
each set of threads as shown in Plate XII, Figures A
and B. Begin on the same side as the finished heading.
Weave one inch with the white chenille in the same
manner as with the carpet warp; three rows of rose
chenille, two rows white chenille, seven rows rose chenille, two rows white chenille, three rows rose chenille,
nine inches white chenille, repeat the border (three rows
rose, two rows white, seven rows rose, two rows white
and three rows rose); then weave one inch white chenille and one-half inch natural colored carpet warp for
the heading as in the beginning.

When removing the material from the loom, begin in
the middle of the loom, with the end that is nearest you.
Slip off the outside edge loop (1) (See Plate XIII, Figure A) and with a large needle pull the loop threads
toward the top and to the right at (2) so the thread
that formed the loop at (1) is an even edge. Pull the
loop at (3) until the loop at (2) comes down and is

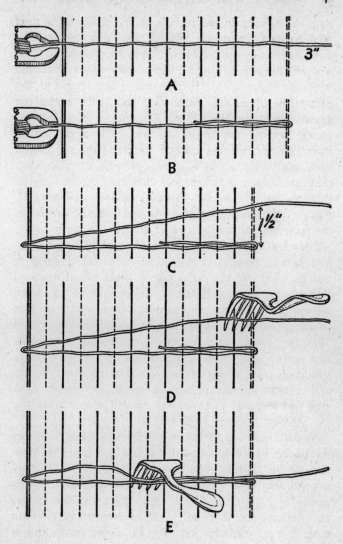

PLATE XII

even with the top edge. Continue across the loom to the right edge, fastening the end by running it down beside the next to the last warp thread. Now at the center (1) pull up the warp thread at (4) and proceed in the same manner to the left until the left edge is reached, and fasten the end by running it down beside the next to the last warp thread on the left.

Use a running stitch for the edge of the face cloth as shown in Plate XIII, Figure B, and hem.

## BEACH SANDAL

### (See Plate XIV, Figure A)

EQUIPMENT:

    Fellowcrafters School Loom
    3 Shuttles
    Heddle Rods
    Board for making Heddles
    "C" Clamp
    Zero Spring Punch, Small
    Space Marker as used in leatherwork
    1 Needle, 2" Tapestry
    "C" Clamp
    Fork or Forked Stick

MATERIALS:

    Warp— Natural Carpet Warp, 50 yds.
            Gray Carpet Warp, 50 yds.
            Natural colored Mercerized 10/2 Cotton, 1 tube for the heading.
    Weft— Perleen, two colors, 1 tube each or
            Strand Cotton, two colors, 1 tube each
    Soles— Latex of proper size to allow the cutting out of four soles for each pair of sandals.

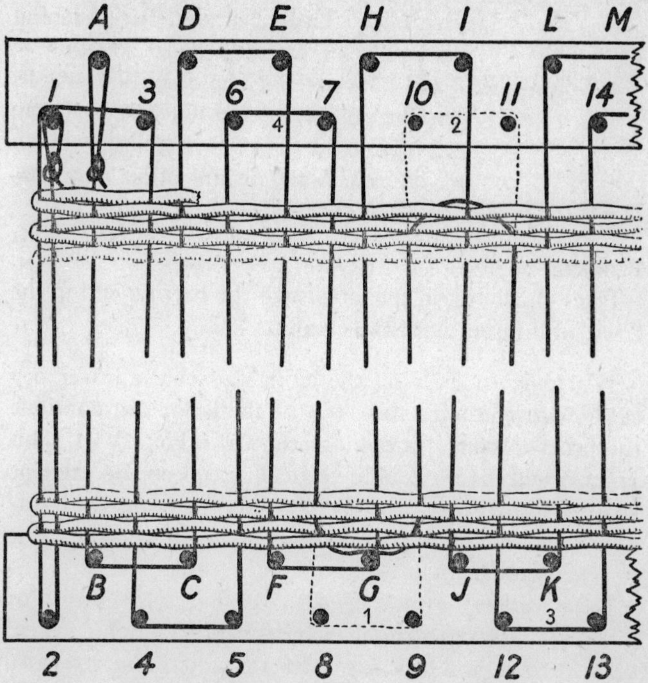

A

B

PLATE XIII

Deluxe Gimp Lacing, 3 yds., for fastening
the two soles of each sandal together.

Color— Red and blue-green. (The described process
uses the colors red and blue-green. If tan
and orange, or light blue and light yellow
are desired, these, or any other combinations, can be used.)

PROCESS:

Place the loom on the table with the narrow end in the
front, and fasten with the clamp.

*Warping:* In warping the loom start at the lower peg
at the extreme left at the top of the loom and continue
the process from this point as shown in Plate VIII. This
process will give a double vertical thread on the extreme
left and right sides of each pattern. The loom is of sufficient size to allow two separate strips of weaving, one
for each sandal.

Each vertical group of the weaving will consist of
thirty-three threads which will include the double thread
on the right and the left sides for additional strength.
The seventeen threads of the first color form the double
thread at the left and finish with a double thread at the
right. Warp sixteen single threads of the second color,
beginning at the double thread left edge of the loom and
ending at the right double thread.

*Weaving:* Weave a half-inch heading of the natural
colored mercerized cotton. Begin and end the mercerized
heading as shown in Plate XII, Figure B. Wind two
shuttles of red and one shuttle of blue-green.

Take a shuttle of red, open the next shed, weaving it
through eight threads from the left edge, bring up

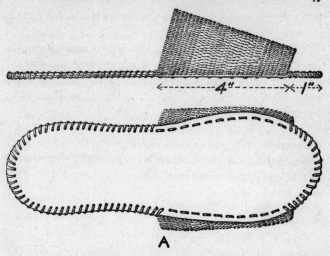

A

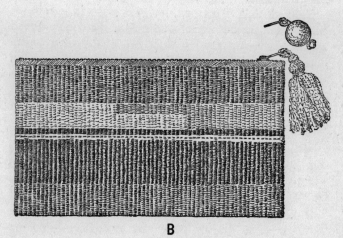

B

PLATE XIV

through the warp, and leave a three-inch end for fastening (See Plate XV, Figure A).

Take the other shuttle of red and, after counting eight warp threads in from the right edge, enter the shuttle, using the same shed, weaving through to the right edge. Leave a three-inch end for fastening (See Plate XV, Figure A).

Take a shuttle of blue-green, enter the shed between the eighth and the ninth warp threads from the right edge, and pass it through until it meets the first shuttle of the red, and bring it out at this point (Plate XV, Figure A). Open the second shed and fasten all three ends as shown in Plate XV, Figure A.

For a simple means of joining two weft threads of different colors in the middle of a piece of weaving (Plate XV, Figure C), lay the first shuttle of red to the left (Plate XV, Figure B), open your second shed, take the second shuttle of the red, pass it through the shed and up through the warp between the seventh and eighth threads from the right edge. Take the third shuttle, the blue-green, put it through the loop of red from the first shuttle and pass it through the shed toward the right and out between the seventh and eighth warp threads from the right edge. Take the first shuttle and pass it through the shed to the left edge of the warp. Beat all down with a fork or a forked stick.

Repeat this process by passing the blue-green shuttle under "left red shuttle thread" loop, and then passing the "right red shuttle" from the right through the loop of blue-green, until the strip is eight inches long. (Plate XV, Figure D.) Fasten the three-inch end of each color. Finish by weaving a half-inch heading of mercerized cotton.

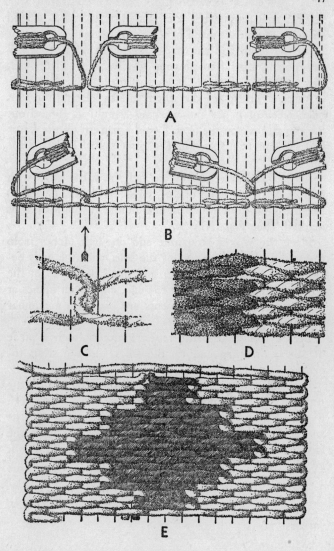

A

B

C

D

E

PLATE XV

This strip completes one sandal strap and a second strap is, of course, made in the same manner. Remove it from the loom and run irregularly each edge with any fine cotton thread to prevent fraying. (See Plate XIII, Figure B.)

Make a pattern for the sandal sole by placing the foot on a piece of paper' and marking around it. Round out the toe and widen the heel. Lay the pattern on the Latex and cut out two soles for the right sandal and two for the left.

Mark three-sixteenths of an inch from the edge with a space marker around one of the soles. Put the two soles for the same foot together and punch through both as marked. (See Plate XIV.)

Place the woven strap one and one-half inches from the middle of the toe-end of the sole, with the ends between the soles, leaving four and one-half inches of the woven part showing at the toe-end, and seven inches at the instep. These measurements are based on a number five or six shoe.

Before lacing, take the tapestry needle with a piece of string or warp and tie the soles and the strap together.

For lacing, begin at one edge of the strap, using the running stitch through the woven part (See Plate XIV, Figure A), and an over and over stitch around the toe and heel. Fasten the end by running it back between the lacing of the soles and out through the edge, cutting it even with the edge.

## PURSE

*(See Plate XIV, Figure B)*

EQUIPMENT:

 Fellowcrafters School Loom
 3 Shuttles
 Heddle Rods
 Board for making Heddle
 "C" Clamp
 Fork or Forked Stick

MATERIALS:

 Natural Cotton Warp, 25 yds.
 Gray Cotton Warp, 25 yds.
 Wool Medium, 2 one-ounce skeins, and a dark value
  of the principal color
 Two Light Colors for Pattern, one-half ounce each
 Zipper, 7"
 Silk for the lining, 8" × 14"
 Cloth for the stiffening of the pocket, $3\frac{1}{2}$" × $7\frac{1}{2}$"

COLORS:

 The purse (Plate XIV, Figure B) was made of blue
  Laurel with red and gray Yorkshire yarn for
  the pattern.

PROCESS:

*Warping:* Use fifty-four alternating colored warp
threads, beginning two inches from the right edge of
the loom with a double edge thread and ending at the
left edge with a double edge thread.

*Weaving:* Weave one-half inch of fine gray mercerized cotton for the heading. With the shuttle of medium
blue yarn, weave one inch plain weaving. Start the pat-

tern from the right with the shuttle of gray yarn. Count twenty-four warp threads and bring the shuttle up through the warp and leave a three-inch end for fastening. Pass the shuttle of red yarn through the same shed and bring it up through the warp beside the gray. Join the two threads (Plate XV, Figure C). Change the shed and repeat for one-fourth inch, leaving both shuttles at the right and the left edges, the gray yarn at the right and the red yarn at the left. Open the next shed, take the gray yarn from the right, through and up between the forty-first and the forty-second threads, then the red yarn from the left, up through the same space, and join. Continue this weave for three-eighths of an inch. Weave:

> three-sixteenths of an inch dark blue
> two rows of gray
> two rows of red
> two rows of gray
> one inch of dark blue
> one and one-half inches of medium blue
>     (This is the bottom of the bag.)
> one inch of dark blue
> two rows of gray
> two rows of red
> two rows of gray
> three-sixteenths of an inch dark blue

For the pattern on the second side of the purse, take the gray in from the right and up between the forty-first and the forty-second threads. Take the red from the left up through the same space and join. Continue this weave for three-eighths of an inch. Leave both shuttles on the edges, gray at the right, red at the left.

Bring the gray in from the right edge twenty-four threads, and up through the warp, then the red in the same shed from the left edge and up beside the gray, and join (Plate XV, Figure C). Continue this for one-quarter of an inch. Weave one inch medium blue and finish with one-half inch heading of gray mercerized cotton.

Remove from the loom (See Plate XIII, Figure A).

*Making up the Purse:* Fit the lining to the size of the woven piece making a three and one-half inch tuck in one side for the pocket. Cut the cloth for stiffening of pocket three and one-half inches by seven and one-half inches. Slip it in the tuck, and stitch by hand or machine, one-eighth of an inch from the edge.

Sew the zipper to the lining as near the edge of the zipper as possible. Sew the sides of the lining. Sew the sides of the bag by putting the edges together so the pattern matches, beginning at the edge of the medium blues, taking a stitch through the weft loop on one edge, then through a stitch of the weft loop on the other edge, continuing until the middle of the bottom is reached. Slip the bag over the lining and blind stitch to the zipper.

Either a tassel of wool, or a bead, should be fastened to the slide of the zipper (See Plate XIV, Figure B). If a bead is used, take a second small bead, pass the wool through the big bead, through the slide of the zipper, then through the small bead to hold it, and tie to the first end so that the knot will slip within the big bead.

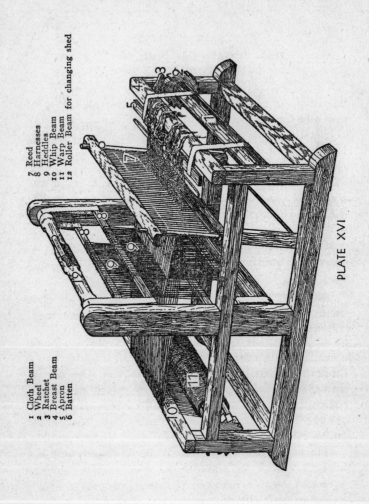

1 Cloth Beam
2 Wheel
3 Ratchet
4 Breast Beam
5 Apron
6 Batten

7 Reed
8 Harnesses
9 Heddles
10 Whip Beam
11 Warp Beam
12 Roller Beam for changing shed

PLATE XVI

# CHAPTER V

## Two-Harness Table Looms

### (See Plate XVI)

THE two-harness table looms are made in three sizes, the smallest offering a maximum weaving width of eight inches; the next, or intermediate, a maximum weaving width of twelve inches, and the largest, a maximum weaving width of eighteen inches. Of course, the weaving can be as long as desired. The eight-inch table loom is used in the weaving of small articles such as scarfs and purses; the twelve-inch loom for scarfs, luncheon sets, and hand towels. In addition to the smaller articles of the narrow looms, the eighteen-inch loom is used for pillow tops and knitting bags.

All types of weaving materials can be used on these looms including cotton, mercerized cotton, linen, wool, silk, and rayon.

### THE WARP CHAIN

The warp chain is made by winding on a frame (See Plate XVII, Figure A) the threads which will run lengthwise on the loom. After winding, these threads are taken from the frame and finger crocheted into a long chain, called the warp chain.

The first step in all weaving is the process of warping, which is done in the same manner with whatever material is chosen. As an example of the process of making a warp chain, use a count of one hundred threads, six yards in length. To make a six yard warp: Tie the two ends of

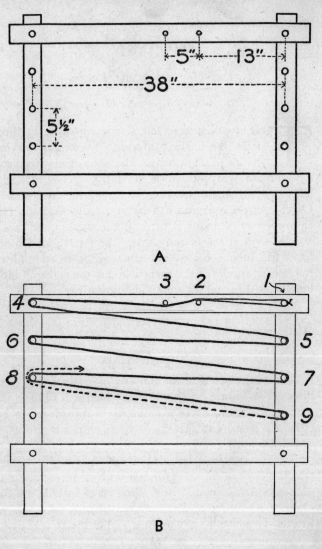

A

B

PLATE XVII

thread together, one from each tube (or spool), and place the knot over peg 1. (Plate XVII, Figure B.) With the knot on the outside of the peg, bring them together and carry them over peg 2, under peg 3, over peg 4, across and over pegs 5, 6, 7, 8, 9. This will be the end of the warp chain—and gives two warp threads, six yards long. Now reverse the process and carry the threads across and under pegs 8 (Plate XVII, Figure B), 7, 6, 5, 4, and over peg 3, under peg 2, and then from under peg 2 straight across under peg 1. This makes a warp of four threads, six yards long. Continue this process until there are twenty-five double warp threads crossing each other each time they pass between pegs 2 and 3. This crossing of threads is called the *Cross* or the *Lease* (Plate XVII, Figure A).

*Counting Warp Threads:* Find the center of a piece of cord or tape, tie it around the twenty-five double threads (fifty single) using a square knot, and allow the ends of this knot to hang down until the second group of twenty-five double threads is made (See Plate XVIII, Figure B), then tie the ends around this other group. A method of counting these threads is shown in Plate XVIII, Figure C: insert the first two fingers of the left hand on either side of the cross and count these, two at a time, with the right hand.

*Tying Warp:* With heavy cord, tie together the warp threads on the top of peg 2 and also the threads on peg 3. The third tie comes on the outside of peg 1 and the fourth tie on the outside of peg 9.

*Removing Warp from the Frame and Chaining It:* The warp is now ready to be removed from the warp frame. Begin at peg 9; take hold of the loop of warp threads around peg 9 with the right hand, and with the left hand

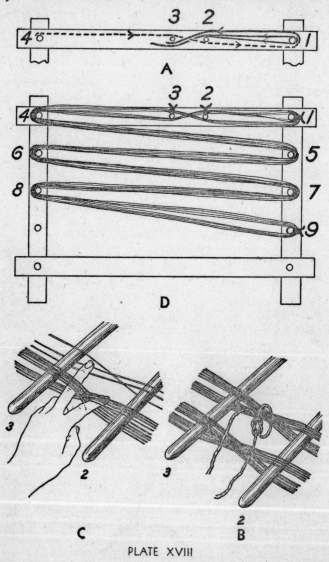

PLATE XVIII

take hold of the entire chain, that is, all threads passing around peg 9 (See Plate XIX, Figure A). Holding this group of threads in the left hand, slide the thumb and fingers of the right hand through the loop and take hold of the entire group of warp threads and bring them through the loop (Plate XIX, Figure B). Continue this process, which is a crochet stitch made with the fingers instead of with a hook. When the tie above peg 3 is reached (See Plate XVIII, Figure D), pull the entire first end of the warp through this loop which will hold it from separating or tangling until you are ready to use it. (Plate XIX, Figure C.)

*Tying the Warp on the Loom* (See Plate XX, Figure A): Slip the end of the warp out at the loop last made, and tie the loop to the breast beam (Plate XX, Figure A, a). Take two sticks, called the Lease Sticks (Plate XX, Figure A, b and c), and insert them through the warp chain at the lease peg positions 2 and 3, (See Plate XVIII, Figure D), leaving about a quarter of an inch space between the sticks.

On Plate XX, Figure A, the lease stick taking the place of peg 2 is "c," and the lease stick in place of peg 3 is "b."

Tie "b" to the breast beam near each end of the stick.

Tie "c" to the top of the batten in two places directly opposite to the place where "b" is tied to the breast beam.

Tie the batten to the sides of the loom so it is in a vertical position, to facilitate the threading of the reed.

Cut the end of the warp chain at "d" which was the beginning of the warp chain.

Untie the end of the cord used to tie the groups of the warp threads in counting, and release the outside group

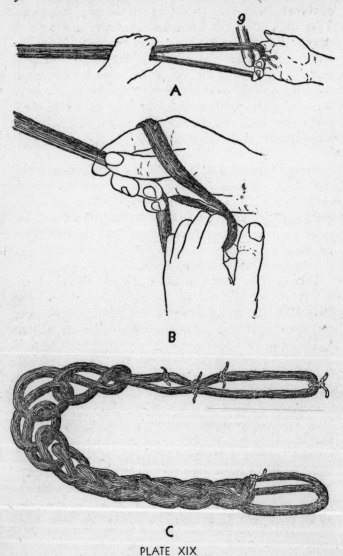

A

B

C

PLATE XIX

of threads. Notice the cross between the two lease sticks. Take the first thread from the right edge and hook it through the dent in the reed where the right side of the weaving will come (See Plate XX, Figure B). Take the next two threads at the left of the edge threads, hook them through the next left dent in the reed in the same way, then the third, and so on, until all are hooked, putting two through the last dent which will be at the left edge.

*Threading the Loom:* Consider the harness nearest the reed at the front of the loom as No. 1, and the harness at the back as No. 2. This designation will be used after the loom (See Plate XVI) has been turned around, because the next step in threading the loom is done from the back.

Turn the loom completely around.

Take the first double thread at the left side and hook it through the first left heddle on harness No. 1. (See Plate XXI, Figure A.) Take the next thread at the right and hook it through the first left heddle on harness No. 2. Take the next thread at the right and hook it through the second heddle from the left on harness No. 1. Continue this process. After a group of about twelve threads has passed through the heddles, their loose ends hanging down, it is wise to tie them together in a loose knot, to prevent them from slipping out of the heddles. Also, it is helpful to tie the loose ends in this manner, as one may thread the loom a part at a time, which often happens when the work is done at intervals. Now take a group of twelve threads, put the ends together, and carry them under the stick held by the tapes on the back warp beam called the apron (See Plate XXI,

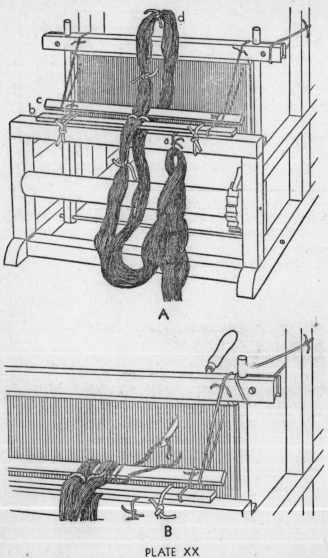

A

B

PLATE XX

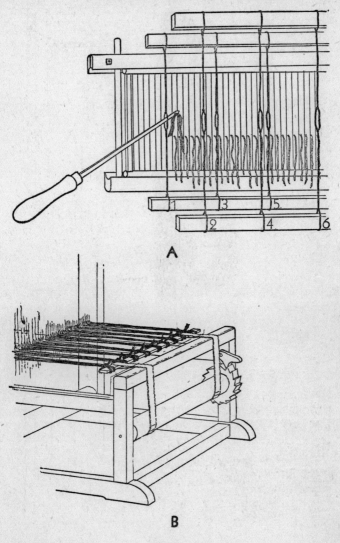

A

B

PLATE XXI

Figure B and Plate XXII, Figure A, 1). Divide the ends, carry half around to the right and half to the left (Plate XXII, Figure A, 2), bringing both groups up and tying them in a single knot (Plate XXII, Figure A, 3).

*Winding Warp on the Warp Beam:* Cut all the cords, (holding the warp to the breast beam) the lease sticks, and so forth, on the front of the loom. Unchain about one yard of warp. Comb the threads with the fingers and hold part of the warp threads in each hand while a second person slowly turns the warp beam.

Place a thin stick parallel to the warp beam, between the beam and the threads that are passing over it. This stick helps to overcome unevenness caused by the knots that have just been tied. Place these sticks during the winding to maintain evenness as shown in Plate XXIII, Figure A, 1, 2, 3, 4, 5, 6, 7, 8, and Figure B. As the winding is completed, care should be taken to wind slowly, as the ends of the warp threads are to be tied to the apron attached to the cloth beam. (See Plate XXIII, Figure C.)

*Tying Warp to the Cloth Beam:* Tying the warp ends to the beam is similar to that of tying the first warp thread to the warp beam (See Plate XXII, Figure B and Plate XXIII, Figure C). The warp threads are lifted to form a shed by turning the top roller beam (See Plate XVI) from which the harnesses are hung. One shed is opened by turning the handle forward and the other shed is opened by turning the handle backward.

*Weaving—How to Judge:* Description of processes often seem uninteresting because of necessary detail— and it is helpful for the beginner to examine closely samples of good weaving. Observation will usually show a double warp thread at each side of the weaving, and

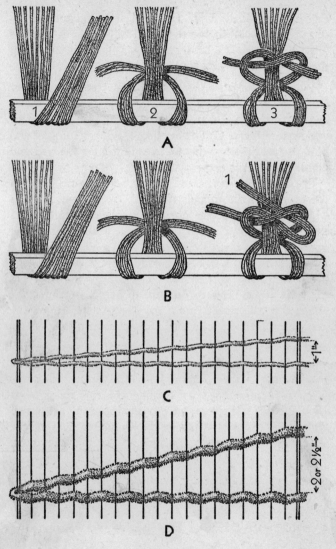

A

B

C

D

PLATE XXII

also that weft threads are turned under so as not to appear on the right side. The ability to determine good weaving is quickly developed by observing the evenness of the distance between the weft threads in the different areas of the weaving, and also by the evenness of the selvage.

*Heading:* At the beginning and the ending of all weaving, it is necessary to form an inch heading for which any fine cotton thread may be used. A heading has a twofold purpose, first, it prevents the newly woven material from fraying, and second, it serves as a fine edge for the inside of the hem.

*Weaving:* Open the shed by turning the roller beam handle forward and put one of the lease sticks through. Open the second shed by turning the roller beam handle backward and put the shuttle of heading through from the left to the right. Leave a three-inch end for fastening.

Weft thread ends are finished by passing around the double edge thread and back into the shed (See Plate XII, Figure B). When several colors are used, care must be taken to pass the end back into a shed of its own color.

The slant of the weft thread is very important in weaving, for on this depends a good edge. If the shuttle is not passed back and forth with a certain consistency of looseness of the weft thread, the edges will either be pulled in too tightly or a large loop will appear in them. The tightness or looseness of the weft thread can be made uniform and even by using the free hand to hold lightly the loop end of the yarn at the edge of the material as the shuttle is passed through. A slant that leaves the thread one inch from the weaving (See Plate XXII, Figure C) is enough when a fine thread, either 20/2 cot-

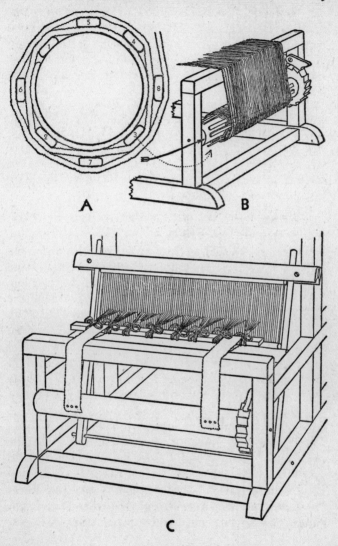

A          B

C

PLATE XXIII

ton or fine linen is used. For No. 3 Pearl Cotton or
coarser thread, there should be a slant of two or two and
a half inches from the weft thread to the edge of the
weaving. (Plate XXII, Figure D.)

*Removing the Weaving from the Loom:* Wind the
weaving on the cloth beam until the heading reaches the
breast beam. Begin at the right of the loom, and cut the
warp threads about one-half inch above the heading (See
Plate XXIV, Figure A). Tie the warp threads in a loose
knot (Plate XXIV, Figure B). After all the warp threads
have been cut and tied, (Plate XXIV, Figure C), release
the rachet, (See Plate XVI), and unwind the weaving
from the cloth beam. Untie the knots by pulling on the
short end of the warp thread, (See Plate XXII, Figure
B, 1).

*Running the Heading:* To check the raveling of the
weft threads before hemstitching, the heading is always
finished by running with a fine cotton thread (Plate
XIII, Figure B). Hold the material with the warp ends
up, and sew back and forth, zigzag, from the right to the
left. Fasten the end of the thread by running into and
along the selvage. Each time the running stitch comes to
the outside edge carry it around the next to the top
weft thread. This keeps the top weft thread in place
until the entire edge is finished. When the zigzag running stitch is down in the weaving, turn it at different
points, to return toward the top edge. This turning in
the weft threads of the heading prevents any separating
strain.

*Hemstitching:* (See Plate XXV, Figures C, D, and E.)
Turn in the heading, and also the hem, so that the edge

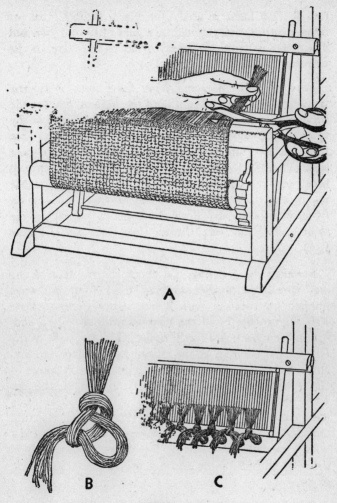

A

B          C

PLATE XXIV

comes on one of the weft threads and baste evenly, following the weft thread across the width of the weaving. Hold the turned-in edge of the thread uppermost, and work from the right to the left. With a needle, pull the weft thread above and next to the hem, and make a small loop about a half inch from the right edge. Cut this thread and turn it in at the right corner of the hem. Thread a needle with sewing cotton and close the narrow hem width at the side, using an overhand stitch from the extreme right corner up to the top where the hemstitching begins. With a needle, pick up two warp threads, (Plate XXV, Figure C), and after passing the thread around them, draw them down firmly to the hem edge, pulling the two threads together as one thread. Again pass the needle around these same two threads, (Plate XXV, Figure D), and sew through the hem between each group of two warp threads. This process is known as single hemstitching. If a double hemstitch is desired, use the same process, sewing into the first double weft thread above the hem. To prevent the closing of the space between the weft threads, it is suggested that the threads be cut and pulled out a half inch at a time. Care should be taken to allow a half inch of the weft thread to be turned in at the left end of the hem as in the beginning of the hemstitching.

*Sewed Fringe:* Hold the weaving in the left hand with the fringe end up and, with a needle of white cotton, run with fine stitch from a point about a half inch down the right selvage up to a point at which the fringe is to be sewed (Plate XXV, Figure A). Pass the needle twice around two or more of the fringe threads, (Plate XXV, Figure B), and draw tightly. Before sewing the fringe to

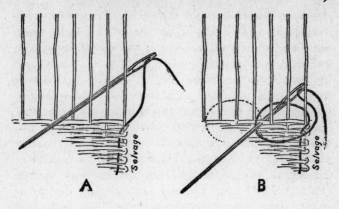

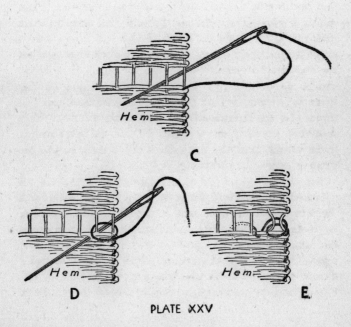

PLATE XXV

the weft, pass the needle through the loop making the first group of fringe threads. Repeat this process across the weaving, and fasten at the left edge by running the thread down the selvage for one-half inch. The number of threads, forming a group in the fringe, depends upon the material and the preference of the weaver; small groups of thread tend to make a fringe edge close and even.

*Tied Fringe:* (See Plate XXVI.) Place the weaving on a table, with a weight to hold it in place, and with the heading hanging over the edge. Begin one inch from the edge at the right, and cut through the white threads of the heading, taking care not to cut the warp threads. Pull out the short white threads at the right of the cut. Take the four right warp threads in the left hand, hold them between the thumb and first and second finger, (Plate XXVI, Figure A), bring them forward around the back of the first and second fingers; hold the ends with the thumb, (Figure B), and take them through the loop thus formed (Figure C), and back under the left thumb (Figure D). With the thumb and the first finger of the right hand take hold of the lower edge of the loop and pull it to the right (Figure E); swing the loop up in a vertical position under the left thumb and the first finger (Figure F). With the right thumb and forefinger pull the end down until the knot at the edge of the weaving is tight and close to the woven edge (Figure G). Continue with the next four threads to the left, and so on, across the weaving.

To hold the weft threads on the edge of the weaving in place until you are ready to tie the fringe, cut and

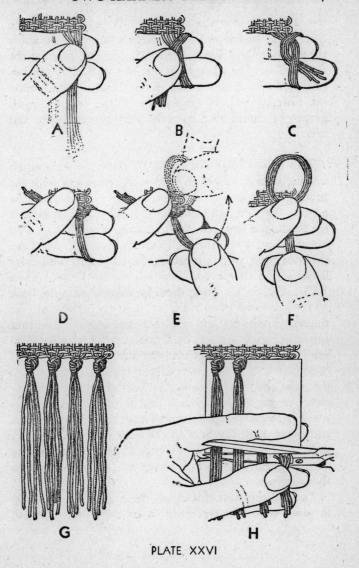

A    B    C

D    E    F

G    H

PLATE XXVI

pull out only about a half-inch of the heading at one time.

When twelve or fifteen threads from the left edge, take out all the remaining threads of the heading and, from the left edge, tie and knot. If the count does not come even, three or five threads may be used for a group.

To cut the fringe, take a card the length desired for the fringe; place the card with two knot groups over and two knot groups under it (Figure H). Hold with the left hand and cut the four knots of fringe at the lower edge of the card. Then take the next four knots and cut in a like manner. This will give an even fringe length across the weaving.

## MERCERIZED COTTON TOWEL

EQUIPMENT:

    Two-Harness Table Loom, 13″ with a 15 dent reed
    Hook for threading
    2 Shuttles
    Warp Frame
    Spool Rack

MATERIALS:

    Warp— Mercerized Cotton, 10/2, White or Natural
    Weft— Mercerized Cotton, 10/2, White or Natural
    Heading— Cotton, 20/2, White
    Border— Strand Cotton
    (As very small amounts are required for the borders two skeins of D.M.C. or other fast-colored embroidery cotton may be used.)

PROCESS:

*Warping:* The length of the warp will depend upon the desired length of the towel. In order to avoid unnecessary waste of warp thread, several towels can be made in one continuous operation. The towel described is twenty-four inches long. Nine or ten inches of additional warp are required for tying the warp before the weaving begins. If one towel only is made, a yard and one-half of warp is necessary, as about half a yard of the warp should be left tied on the loom, (See Plate XXIV, Figure C), so that re-threading will not be necessary when the loom is used again. A six yard warp makes five towels, or if two or three are woven in one continuous piece, six yards will make six towels.

The number of threads in the warp chain depends on the width of the towel. If the desired width is twelve inches finished, it will be necessary to make the warp thirteen inches wide in the reed, because all hand weaving draws in slightly in the weaving, tightens up after removal from the loom, and has some shrinkage in laundering. Thus, for the described towel three hundred and ninety-two (392) threads are needed in the warp chain. The reed has fifteen dents to an inch, and two threads through each dent. Multiply the width, (13″) by the number of threads per inch (30) and add two additional threads for the double thread on each edge which forms the selvage.

Place two tubes of mercerized cotton, 10/2, on the spool rack, (See Glossary), and set the rack on the floor below the lease pegs, two and three, on the warp frame.

For making the warp chain, see pages 54, 56, and 58: Plate XVII, Figures A and B; Plate XVIII, Figures A, B, C, and D; Plate XIX, Figures A, B, and C.

For tying the warp on the loom, see page 60; Plate XX, Figure A.

For threading the loom, see page 60; Plate XX, Figure B.

For winding the warp on the warp beam, see page 65; Plate XXIII, Figures A and B.

For tying the warp to the cloth beam, see page 63, Plate XXII, Figure B.

*Weaving:* Weave a heading of one inch cotton, 20/2. Wind together on a shuttle two threads of the white cotton, 10/2. Weave four inches, double thread, which will give the effect of a basket weave, (Plate V, Figure D), at the end and the hem.

For a simple border this grouping of the threads is suggested:

One row of color
Two rows of white
Two rows of color
Two rows of white
Six rows of color
Two rows of white
Two rows of color
Two rows of white
One row of color

After finishing the border, weave fifteen inches of the double white cotton for the center of the towel. The border is repeated and four inches more of the double white threads are woven for the second end and the hem. Weave one-half inch of the cotton, 20/2, for the heading.

For the weaving, see page 63, Plate XXII, Figures C, and D.

For removing the weaving from the loom, see page 67, XXIV, Figures A, and B.

For running the heading, see page 43, Plate XIII, Figure B.

Turn in the heading on the first heavy thread, and also turn the hem so that the edge comes three-quarters of an inch from the border. Baste evenly by following one of the weft threads across the width of the towel. Sew with an overhand stitch the open ends of the hem.

## STRIPED WOOL SCARF

*(See Plate XXVII, Figure A)*

A scarf can be made individual and distinctive through the harmony or the contrast in colors and the choice of yarns.

EQUIPMENT:

    Two-Harness Table Loom, 9″ with 15 dent reed
    Hook for Threading
    Two Shuttles
    Warp Frame
    Spool Rack

MATERIALS:

    Mercerized Cotton, 20/2, white for the heading
    4 or 5 balls of harmonizing soft wool (Lady Helen)
    (The described scarf is henna and dark henna, a
        blue-green, a tan mixture, and a dark brown for
        the warp. A light tone of henna makes the
        weft.)

PROCESS:

*Warping:* A warp chain of one hundred and twenty-four (124) threads, two yards long, weaves a scarf eight inches wide and forty-five inches long. The colors are combined in stripes:

    Five threads dark brown (two for double edge thread)
    Nine threads dark henna
    Sixteen threads henna
    Six threads blue-green and tan mixed
    Four threads dark brown
    Eight threads dark henna
    Two threads dark brown
    Twenty-four threads henna

(This is the center group of threads)
Two threads dark brown
Eight threads dark henna
Four threads dark brown
Six threads blue-green and tan mixed
Sixteen threads henna
Nine threads dark henna
Five threads dark brown

*Warp Chain:* (See Plates XVII, XVIII, and XIX.) Take the dark brown wool and starting at peg 1, carry it over peg 2, under peg 3, over peg 4 and across to peg 5. This is the end of the warp and gives one thread, two yards long. Reverse the process, across and under peg 4, over peg 3, under peg 2, straight across and around peg 1. Continue this process until five threads of dark brown have been wound on the pegs. The last row will end at peg 5. Tie the dark henna to the brown on the outside of peg 5. Continue the process of winding until there are nine rows of dark henna. The dark henna will end at peg 1. Tie the henna to the dark henna and continue winding until one hundred and twenty-four threads have been wound on the frame. For removing the warp from the frame see page 58. For tying the warp on the loom see page 60, Plate XX, Figure A.

Thread the loom (See page 60) with a double thread for each outside edge. Wind the warp on the warp beam and put in twelve sticks, four at a time, to keep the warp even throughout (See page 65). In winding the wool do not pull, but hold it lightly, as wool stretches easily. Tie the ends to the front apron. Use a stick in the first shed to start the work evenly.

*Weaving:* Make a one-inch heading of white mercerized cotton (See page 64). Begin weaving with the light henna. In weaving with wool keep the last weft thread pulled down to the previous one so they do not touch each other while seen on the loom under tension. This will insure a soft, light scarf.

Weave forty-five inches, and put in a heading of mercerized cotton.

In cutting the scarf off the loom, roll the weaving over until the last heading comes down on the cloth beam. This will leave sufficient of the warp for the fringe, which is cut about six inches long, and also leaves enough warp in front of the reed to be tied to the new warp in later weaving, and thus save re-threading the loom. Untie the threads from the stick that forms the edge of the apron on the cloth beam. For tying the fringe see page 71, Plate XXVI, A to G. Cut the fringe for a man's scarf two and one-half or three inches long; for a woman's, four or five inches long.

## PLAID SCARF

### (See Plate XXVII, Figure B)

The plaid scarf offers another variety of design and, while the pattern seems more involved, the process is the same as for the striped scarf, except that additional shuttles are required and the weaving is broken up by the frequent turning in of the ends.

EQUIPMENT:
   Two-Harness Table Loom, 19" with 15 dent reed
   Hook for Threading
   Four Shuttles
   Warp Frame
   Spool Rack

MATERIALS:
   Mercerized Cotton, 20/2, for Heading

Yorkshire Wool in three colors
Suggested color combinations:
1. Light and dark gray with jade green
2. Light and dark brown with henna (described)
3. Light and dark gray-blue with tan

PROCESS:

*Warping:* Two hundred and one threads are required for a warp chain two and one-quarter yards long, and thirteen inches wide when it is threaded through the reed.

Warp the loom (See page 57), using two threads for each edge and one thread through each dent in the reed. For threading the loom, see page 60.

A—Five threads dark brown
B—Twenty-three threads light brown
C—Eight threads henna
B—Thirteen threads light brown
A—Five threads dark brown
B—Thirty-one threads light brown
C—Eight threads henna
A—Thirteen threads dark brown
     (This is the center of the scarf)
C—Eight threads henna
B—Thirty-one threads light brown
A—Five threads dark brown
B—Thirteen threads light brown
C—Eight threads henna
B—Twenty-three threads light brown
A—Five threads dark brown

The letters indicate warp pattern color as shown on Plate XXVII, Figure B.

*Weaving:* Make a one-inch heading of mercerized cotton, 20/2. Begin with the dark brown wool and weave the same number of rows of each color as there are in the warp:

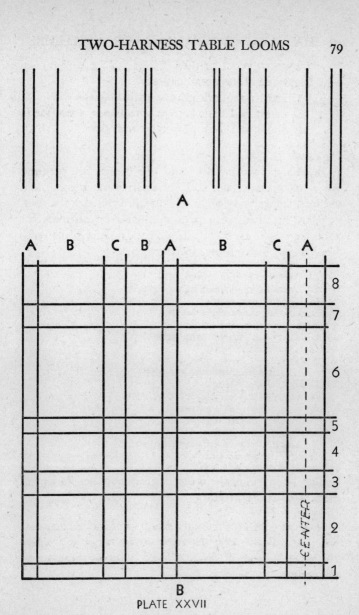

A

B

PLATE XXVII

1—Five rows dark brown
2—Twenty-three rows light brown
3—Eight rows henna
4—Thirteen rows light brown
5—Five rows dark brown
6—Thirty-one rows light brown
7—Eight rows henna
8—Thirteen rows light brown

The numbers indicate weaving pattern shown on Plate XXVII, Figure B.

Continue repeating this group until one-half the length of the scarf is woven. Four repeats will make about twenty-eight inches, which, when taken off the loom, will shrink to about twenty-five inches. Reverse the pattern at the center length of the scarf, omitting the light brown of thirteen rows so that the pattern will not vary at the center. Weave:

7—Eight rows henna
6—Thirty-one rows light brown
5—Five rows dark brown
4—Thirteen rows light brown
3—Eight rows henna
2—Twenty-three rows light brown
1—Five rows dark brown

The numbers indicate weaving pattern shown on Plate XXVII, Figure B.

Repeat this group four times, then make a half-inch heading of mercerized cotton, 20/2. Take off the loom leaving enough warp for the fringe (See page 77). Tie the fringe with four threads for each knot (See page 71).

## LINEN RUNNER (STRIPED)

The weaver must determine in advance where the runner will be most attractively and usefully placed.

This decides the size and the colors for the weaving. Colors which would combine harmoniously on maple, such as, three values of natural colored flax, lose their appeal when placed on mahogany. The runner described is of Russian importation and suggests maple or a light wood as an interesting setting.

EQUIPMENT:

> Two-Harness Table Loom, 19″ with a 15 dent reed
> Hook for Threading
> One Shuttle
> Warp Frame
> Spool Rack

MATERIALS:

> Warp— Two 2-oz. tubes middle value Pussywillow
>              Linen, 16/3
>              Two 2-oz. tubes darkest value Ascot Brown
>              Linen, 16/3
> Weft— Two 2-oz. tubes middle value Natural Linen
>              16/3

PROCESS:

*Warping:* A runner, about seventeen inches wide, needs two hundred and sixty-six threads for the warp chain. Warp the loom using two threads for each edge and one thread through each dent of the reed, (See page 60).

Pattern:

| Group of Stripes | Four threads of the lightest value |
| | Four threads of the darkest value |
| | Eight threads of the lightest value |
| | Four threads of the darkest value |
| | Four threads of the lightest value |
| Plain Band | Twenty-four threads of the darkest value |

Group
of
Stripes
{
Four threads of the lightest value
Four threads of the darkest value
Eight threads of the lightest value
Four threads of the darkest value
Four threads of the lightest value
}

Plain Band    Twenty-four threads of the darkest value

Continue until there are six groups of the stripes with five of the plain bands between them.

*Weaving:* Make a one-inch heading of fine linen. The same weight linen is used for both the warp and the weft, which gives a rough, almost basket weave, effect. Make a one-inch heading at the other end. For removal from the loom (See page 67). Finish by making a one-half inch hem (See page 75).

## LINEN GUEST TOWEL

The described linen guest towel is of a soft weave which resembles scrim and can be used attractively as a tray cloth since its size fits individual breakfast or luncheon plate mats.

EQUIPMENT:

Two-Harness Table Loom, 13″, with a 15 dent reed
Hook for Threading
Two Shuttles
Warp Frame
Spool Rack

MATERIALS:

Warp— Natural Linen, 40/2
Weft— Natural Linen, 2-oz. tube
(A small amount of violet, blue, green, yellow and orange linen for the borders.)

PROCESS:

*Warping:* Use three hundred and ninety-two threads

for the warp chain and make it four, six, or ten yards long, depending upon the number of towels to be woven. Plan on three towels for every two yards, if left on the loom until all are woven, otherwise, on one towel for each yard, if each is cut off separately.

The loom is threaded for plain weaving, with two threads in each dent of the reed. (See page 60.)

*Weaving:*
One-half inch fine linen for the heading
One inch natural linen

Border
- One-quarter inch violet
- Three-sixteenths of an inch blue
- One-eighth of an inch green
- Three-sixteenths of an inch yellow
- One-quarter of an inch orange

Thirteen inches natural linen
Repeat border
One inch natural linen
One-half inch fine linen for the heading
Three other combinations for borders are given below:

1
- Three-eighths of an inch orange
- One-quarter of an inch yellow
- One-eighth of an inch green

2
- Three-eighths of an inch violet
- One-quarter of an inch blue
- One-eighth of an inch green

3
- One-quarter of an inch orange
- One-eighth of an inch yellow
- Three-eighths of an inch orange
- One-eighth of an inch yellow
- One-quarter of an inch orange

For the finish make a sewed fringe in units of three threads (See page 69, Plate XXV, Figures A and B).

## COTTON CHENILLE BAG

### (See Plate XXVIII)

Cotton chenille comes in such a variety of colors that anyone can easily have a good color harmony in the pattern for a knitting or a street bag. In the bag, as shown, a warm yellow, a deep yellow-orange, with a taupe background are used. The handle is made of black walnut.

EQUIPMENT:

>    Two-Harness Table Loom, 9″ with a 15 dent reed
>    Hook for Threading
>    Three Shuttles
>    Warp Frame
>    Spool Rack

MATERIALS:

>    Warp— Mercerized cotton, No. 10
>    Weft— ½ skein Taupe Chenille
>         Small amount of yellow and yellow-orange.

>>    (On Plate XXVIII the lightest value, of which there are three stripes on each side of the bag, is the yellow. The middle value is the yellow-orange, and the third, or darkest value, the taupe.)

>    Bag Handle—1½″ × 8½″
>    Zipper—8″
>    Lining—Silk or Cotton 10″ × 27″
>    Silk Twist, one spool, to match either the wood of the handle or the background of the bag.

PROCESS:

*Warping:* A warp chain of one hundred and thirty-seven threads is required. A two yard warp will make

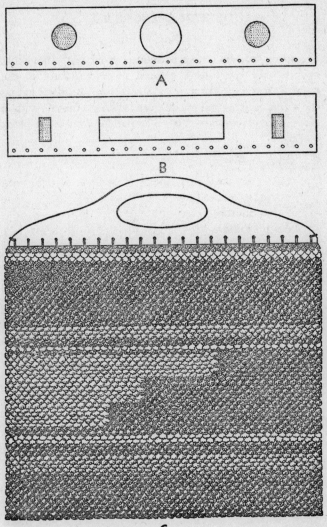

A

B

C

PLATE XXVIII

two bags. Warp the loom (Page 57), using two threads for each edge and one thread for each dent in the reed.

*Weaving:*

> One inch cotton, No. 10 for the heading
> One-half inch taupe chenille
> Two rows yellow chenille
> One and five-eighths inches taupe chenille
> Three-eighths inch yellow-orange
> Two rows taupe
> One row yellow
> One row taupe
> Two inches taupe and orange

For the pattern use two shuttles and follow the same method of joining two colors as shown on Plate XV, Figures C and D. Start in from the right edge with the shuttle of orange chenille and bring the shuttle up between the ninetieth and ninety-first warp threads for joining. Count the double edge thread as one. Start the shuttle, with the taupe chenille, in from the left edge and bring it up between the same two threads; pass the orange chenille through the loop of the taupe chenille; change the shed, and continue for six rows of each color. This will bring both shuttles to the outside edge. Open the next shed, and bring the orange chenille in and up between the fifty-seventh and fifty-eighth warp threads from the right. Bring the shuttle with the taupe from the left, in the same shed and up between the same two threads, joining as before, and weaving six rows of each color. Then take the shuttle with the orange, in from the right and up and between the forty-fifth and forty-sixth warp threads from the right, and the shuttle with the taupe from the left and bring up and join as before; weave six rows of each color and continue with the taupe chenille.

Two rows taupe
Two rows yellow
Three rows taupe
Four rows orange
Two and a half inches taupe, for the bottom of the bag
   (One quarter inch marks the middle of the bottom.)

For the other half of the bag, reversing the process, weave as previously directed from the bottom to the top, keeping the orange in the central pattern on the same side so the edges will join properly when folded together, orange to orange and taupe to taupe. Finish the end with a half inch of heading. Remove the weaving from the loom and run the heading with a fine thread. (See Plate XIII, Figure B.)

*Making up the Bag:* Fold the bag and match the pattern along the edges. Begin at the bottom and work up, sewing through the loops of chenille and around the double edge warp threads to within two inches of the top. Turn in the heading so that the first chenille thread forms the edge, and with the same running stitch as used for the edge, sew it down flat against the side of the bag.

Make up the lining, allowing for a five-inch pocket on one side, and a half-inch tuck on each side to sew to the zipper. Also allow for a quarter inch hem on both sides to sew to the outside of the bag. This brings the zipper below the handle and will hold the contents of the bag securely. Now, slip the lining into the bag, and blind stitch the tuck edge of the lining up to the edge of the heading, where the first row of chenille begins.

The handles are sewed on the outside of the top two or three rows of chenille, as shown on Plate XXVIII, Figure C.

### KNITTING OR UTILITY BAG

The basket weave (See Glossary) is used for the described bag.

EQUIPMENT:
>    Two-Harness Table Loom, 19″, with a 15 dent reed
>    Hook for Threading
>    Four Shuttles
>    Warp Frame
>    Spool Rack

MATERIALS:
>    Warp— Mercerized Cotton, No. 3, middle and light
>           values of taupe
>    Weft— Mercerized Cotton, No. 3, light value of
>           taupe
>    Mercerized Cotton, No. 3, soft green
>    Mercerized Cotton, No. 3, dark brown
>    Mercerized Cotton, 20/2, gray, for heading

PROCESS:
*Warping:* Two hundred and fifty-four threads are needed for a two yard warp of the light and medium value of taupe, the two threads alternating. Thread the reed with a double thread for each edge and one thread through each dent. Thread the heddles with two threads in the front harness and two threads in the back harness.

*Weaving:*

>    One-half inch, gray cotton for the heading
>    Five inches, light taupe
>    Three rows, dark brown
>    Two rows, light taupe
>    Four rows, green

Two rows, light taupe
Three rows, dark brown
Nine rows, green
Two rows, light taupe
Fifteen rows, dark brown (Middle of the border)
Two rows, light taupe
Five inches, light taupe for the bottom of the bag

Repeat the border. (For the repeat of the border follow the above in the reverse order.)

Five inches, light taupe
Half-inch, gray cotton for the heading

Remove the weaving from the loom and run the heading. (See Plate XIII, Figure B.)

This type of bag is fitted with a wooden handle for slipping over the arm. Choose an appropriate wood to harmonize with the weaving pattern—maple for a summer bag of light colors, gumwood for taupe and green, and walnut for dark reds.

*Making up the Bag:* Match the stripes on the sides of the bag and back stitch three-eighths of an inch from the edges at the bottom of the bag up to within three inches of the top. Turn the heading on the second row of top threads to the inside of the bag and run with a zigzag stitch (Plate XIII, Figure B).

When cutting the lining, allow for a half-inch margin on the sides. If the bag is sixteen and a half inches wide, off the loom, the lining should be cut seventeen and a half inches wide, with a seven-eighths inch allowance in the length. Cut a section for a pocket and stitch on one side of the lining. Sew the sides of the lining to within three inches of the top making it one-half inch narrower than the actual size of the bag. Place the lining inside of the bag; pin it at the bottom to hold firmly, and turn in the edges evenly at the top, so that it is a little smaller than the outside. Baste and hem to the outside at the top.

The handles are sewed with silk twist to match the outside of the bag as shown on Plate XXVIII. To give shapeliness to the bag and to have it match the handles previously described, fold in the corners of the bag two inches from the top and two inches from the side to form an angle at each side.

### LINEN FLOSS RUNNER

#### (*Plate XXIX*)

Linen floss is another effective material for weaving. The colors chosen for the described runner consist of a warp of white linen, and a pattern of white with two tones of rust.

EQUIPMENT:

    Two-Harness Table Loom, 9″, with a 15 dent reed
    Hook for Threading
    Three Shuttles
    Warp Frame
    Spool Rack

MATERIALS:

    Warp— Rope Linen Floss, white
    Weft— Rope Linen Floss, dark rust
           Rope Linen Floss, light rust
           Rope Linen Floss, white
           Fine Linen, white, for the heading

PROCESS:

*Warping:* Make a warp chain of one hundred and twenty-five threads, two yards long. Thread the loom one thread to each dent of the reed. Plate XXIX shows in draft form (See Glossary) the pattern for the thread-

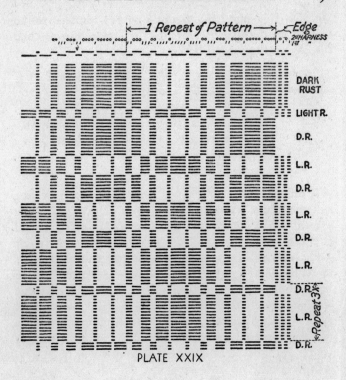

PLATE XXIX

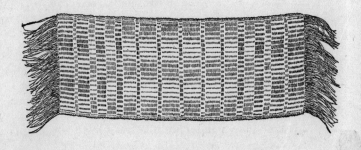

ing. On this plate the figure one (1) represents the threads on the first harness and the figure zero (0) the threads on the second harness:

Edge— 10101.
Pattern— 0000, 1, 00000, 1, 0000, 11, 000, 111, 00, 1111,
0, 11111, 0, 1111, 00, 111, 000, 11, 0000, 1,
00000, (This is the center) 1, 0000, 11, 000,
111, 00, 1111, 0, 11111, 0, 1111, 00, 111, 000,
11, 0000, 1, 00000, 1, 00000, 1, 0000.
Edge— 10101.

*Weaving:* Make a heading. Start with the dark rust and the white, alternate fifteen rows of each. Add one row of white, which will make two rows of white between the dark rust and the light rust, the next color used. Alternate three rows of light rust and three rows of white. Add another row of white. Alternate twelve rows of dark rust and twelve rows of white; add one row of white. Alternate six rows of light rust and six rows of white; add one row of white. Alternate nine rows of dark rust and nine rows of white; add one row of white. Alternate nine rows of light rust and nine rows of white; add one row of white. Alternate six rows of dark rust and six rows of white; add one row of white. Alternate twelve rows of light rust and twelve rows of white; add one row of white.

Alternate the following two patterns three times:

First Pattern—Starting with the dark rust alternate three rows of the dark rust and three rows of the white; add one row of the white.
Second Pattern—Starting with the light rust alternate fifteen rows of the light rust and fifteen rows of the white; add one row of the white.

Now the pattern is repeated, so that the unfinished end matches the finished end. In the following patterns, start with the color as given and alternate with a row of white, also add one row of white between each pattern.

> Three rows of dark rust and three rows of white
> Twelve rows of dark rust and twelve rows of white
> Six rows of dark rust and six rows of white
> Nine rows of light rust and nine rows of white
> Nine rows of dark rust and nine rows of white
> Six rows of light rust and six rows of white
> Twelve rows of dark rust and twelve rows of white
> Three rows of light rust and three rows of white
> Fifteen rows of dark rust and fifteen rows of white

Finish with a heading of fine white linen. For the sewed fringe see page 69, Plate XXV, Figures A and B.

### LINEN LUNCHEON SET
#### (See Plate XXX, Figure A)

A breakfast or luncheon set of six plate mats and a center oblong may be made by combining a mercerized cotton warp with a linen weft or filler. This weaving makes a very attractive and serviceable table set, of sufficient weight to lie flat on a table and present a smartness of appearance upon which any type of glass, china or pottery may be attractively placed. This luncheon set has, at the top and the bottom, borders about an inch wide of soft blue linen running lengthwise.

EQUIPMENT:
> Two-Harness Table Loom, 19″, with a 10 dent reed
> Hook for Threading
> Two Shuttles
> Warp Frame
> Spool Rack
> Needle, 5″, with a curved point

MATERIALS:

Warp— White Mercerized Cotton, 10/2
Weft— White Linen, soft finish
Blue Linen, soft finish
White Mercerized Cotton, 20/2, for the
heading

PROCESS:

*Warping:* Make a warp chain of three hundred and forty-four threads. This allows for a double thread on each edge. A five-yard warp will make six plate mats, eleven inches by sixteen inches, finished, and also an oblong mat for the center of the table, sixteen inches by twenty inches. Thread the loom for plain weaving with two threads to each dent of the reed.

### PLATE MAT

*Weaving:*

One inch white mercerized cotton, 20/2, for the heading
Wind a shuttle with two threads of white linen and weave three inches

Border: Thread the needle with a double blue thread. Open the next shed and needle weave on the upper threads of this shed. (Plate XXX, Figure A.)

Under three threads, over two threads
Under two threads, over two threads

*Repeat eight times.*
Under fourteen threads, over two threads
Under two threads, over two threads

Under three threads
Use a single white thread for a binder

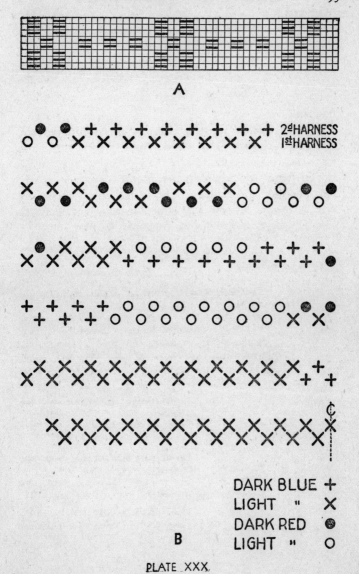

A

2d HARNESS
1st HARNESS

DARK BLUE +
LIGHT " ✕
DARK RED ◉
LIGHT " ○

B

PLATE XXX.

after each blue thread. Repeat the above pattern twice making three rows in all. In the same shed again needle weave the blue linen thread:

Under five threads, over two threads

*Repeat eight times.*

{ Under four threads, over two threads
Under two threads, over two threads
Under two threads, over two threads
Under four threads, over two threads }

Under five threads

Open the pattern shed again using a double blue thread and the white binder between the rows of the pattern:

Under three threads, over two threads

Under two threads, over two threads

Under two threads, over two threads

*Repeat eight times.*

{ Under fourteen threads, over two threads
Under two threads, over two threads }

Under three threads

*Center of the Mat:*

{ Seven and a half inches of double white linen
Repeat the border
Three inches of double white linen
One-half inch white mercerized cotton, 20/2, for the heading }

Run the heading of the mat, (See Plate XIII, Figure B), and hemstitch, (See Plate XXV, Figures C, D, and E).

## OBLONG FOR THE CENTER OF THE TABLE

> One-inch mercerized cotton, 20/2, for the heading
> Four inches of double white linen for the end of the oblong
> Repeat the border as used on the plate mat
> Five rows of double white linen
> Repeat the border
> Twenty inches of double white linen
> Repeat the border
> Five rows of double white linen
> Repeat the border
> Four inches of double white linen
> One-half inch mercerized cotton, 20/2, for the heading

Finish the mats with an inch hem and baste; for the hemstitching, see Plate XXV, Figures C, D, and E.

## INDIAN WEAVE RUNNER

### (Plate XXX, Figure B)

This runner with its wide variation of color, and its highly decorative quality, while much wider than the belts worn in the old days by the Indians, creates a similar effect. Variations of this same runner of a narrower width and of appropriate colors make an interesting wrap-around belt.

EQUIPMENT:

> Two-Harness Table Loom, 13″, with a 15 dent reed
> Hook for Threading
> Three Shuttles
> Warp Frame
> Spool Rack

MATERIALS:

> Warp— Blue-green, light, 10/2

    Blue-green, dark, 10/2
    Light red, neutralized, 10/2
    Dark red, neutralized, 10/2
Weft— Mercerized cotton, 20/2, for the heading
    Blue-green, light, 10/2
    Blue-green, dark, 10/2

PROCESS:

*Warping:* Make a warp chain of two hundred and forty-three threads, two yards long. Thread the reed with two threads in each dent as shown on Plate XXX, Figure B. One thread of dark blue-green on the second harness, one thread of light blue-green on the first harness, one thread of dark blue-green on the second harness, one thread of light blue-green on the first harness; continue until there are eight dark blue-green threads on the second harness and eight light blue-green threads on the first harness, threaded alternately. The threading continues as outlined on Plate XXX, Figure B, using the color as indicated:

    + — For dark blue-green
    × — For light blue-green
    ● — For dark red
    O — For light red

*Weaving:* Start the weaving with one inch of mercerized cotton, 20/2, for the heading. Wind one shuttle with two threads of dark blue-green mercerized cotton, weave two inches. Wind another shuttle with two threads of light blue-green mercerized cotton, weave one and one-quarter inches. Then weave, two inches of the dark blue-green and two and one-half inches of the light blue-green; two inches of the dark blue-green and five inches of the light blue-green; two inches of the dark blue-green for the center of the runner.

The second half of the runner is woven to match the finished end:

> Five inches of light blue-green
> Two inches of dark blue-green
> Two and one-half inches of light blue-green
> Two inches of dark blue-green
> One and one quarter inches of light blue-green
> Two inches of dark blue-green

Finish the weaving with a heading of one-half inch of mercerized cotton, 20/2. For tying the fringe see page 71, Plate XXVI.

## PILLOW COVER
### (*Plate XXXI*)

This pillow cover of colonial blue and white is suggestive of the peasant weaving in its appearance, and offers both sturdiness and quaintness. Also, this weaving is suitable as a chair cushion, or as a table square for the dining-room table between meals.

EQUIPMENT:
> Two-Harness Table Loom, 19″, with a 15 dent reed
> Hook for Threading
> Two-pointed Grooved Shuttles
> Warp Frame
> Spool Rack
> Pointed Stick

MATERIALS:
> Warp— Two 2 oz. tubes Mercerized Cotton, 20/2, colonial blue
> Weft— One 2 oz. tube Mercerized Cotton, 5/2, white

White Mercerized Cotton, 20/2, for the heading

PROCESS:

*Warping:* Make a warp chain of five hundred and sixty-three threads, two yards long. Thread the loom two threads to each dent of the reed.

*Weaving:* Begin with one inch of mercerized cotton, 20/2, for the heading. Weave two and one-quarter inches of white mercerized cotton, 5/2. The pattern (See Plate XXXI) for this pillow cover is made by picking up certain of the upper row of threads on one shed and then on the other with the point of the shuttle.

Begin at the right edge of the loom; pass the shuttle with the white mercerized cotton under thirty-one threads, over three threads, under six threads, over three threads, under six threads, and over three threads. Take a pointed stick and beginning at the left edge, pass it under thirty-one threads, over three threads, under six threads, over three threads, under six threads, and over three threads. While the threads are held in position with the stick, continue across the loom from the right to the left with the shuttle, picking up the threads as held by the stick.

Change the shed, and, beginning at the left edge, pass the shuttle under thirty threads, over four threads, under five threads, over four threads, under five threads, and over four threads. Beginning at the right edge, pick up the threads with a stick, in the same order as picked up with the shuttle from the left.

Plate XXXI shows this pattern clearly; each square on the draft form represents a thread on the first shed, and each line a thread on the second shed.

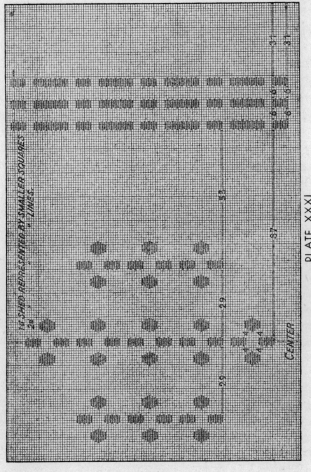

PLATE XXXI

# CHAPTER VI

## Two-Harness Treadle Loom

### (See Plate XXXII)

THE treadle loom differs from the table loom in its operation. By the substitution of pedals for the roller beam to shift the harness, faster weaving is possible because the shed is changed with one foot (or the other) on the pedals, while placing the shuttle for the next row of weft. Its larger size adds ruggedness, which permits harder beating, (See Glossary), and therefore, a broader usage for the making of baby blankets, homespun materials for dresses or suits, and rugs.

### GOLD LUSTER TABLE SQUARE OR PILLOW COVER

The described pillow cover is of Viennese origin. It has an unusual combination of yellow, tan, henna, and gray-green yarns and silks, which give a near metallic effect through the subtle shading of the colors. First used as a pillow cover, but later, because it was woven in one piece, it was ripped at the seams and used as a table cover.

EQUIPMENT:
    Two-Harness Treadle Loom, 36", with a 12 dent reed
    Hook for Threading
    8 Shuttles
    Warp Frame
    Spool Rack

MATERIALS:
    Warp— Colored warp, 20/2, light tan or coffee

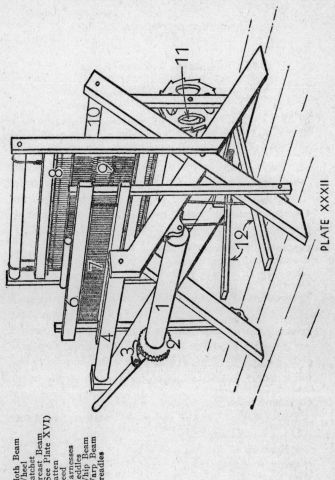

PLATE XXXII

1 Cloth Beam
2 Wheel
3 Ratchet
4 Breast Beam
5 (See Plate XVI)
6 Batten
7 Reed
8 Harnesses
9 Heddles
10 Whip Beam
11 Warp Beam
12 Treadles

Weft— Five tones of henna wool, light to dark
(Number the tones from light to dark 1
to 5)

Silk, Light red-orange
Knitting Chenille, Neutralized orange
Knitting Chenille, Gray-green, light and dark
Mercerized cotton, 20/2 for the heading

PROCESS:

*Warping:* Warp the loom with eight hundred and sixty-six threads for a thirty-six inch width. Thread the loom for plain weaving, with two threads to each dent of the reed, and an extra thread, for each edge.

*Weaving:*

One inch mercerized cotton, 20/2, for the heading
One and one-half inches number 3 henna
Three-sixteenths of an inch number 1 henna
One-fourth of an inch number 3 henna
Two threads number 1 henna
Three threads number 3 henna
One-fourth of an inch number 1 henna
Three-sixteenths of an inch orange silk
Three-eighths of an inch number 5 henna
Three-fourths of an inch number 3 henna
Seven-eighths of an inch number 4 henna
Three-fourths of an inch number 1 henna
One-eighth of an inch orange silk
One-half inch number 5 henna
One-half inch number 3 henna
Two threads orange silk
One-fourth of an inch number 3 henna
Three-sixteenths of an inch number 4 henna
One-fourth of an inch number 1 henna
One inch orange wool
One-eighth of an inch orange silk
One-fourth of an inch number 3 henna
One and one-half inches orange knitting chenille
One-fourth of an inch light gray-green chenille
Three-fourths of an inch orange knitting chenille
Three-eighths of an inch dark gray-green chenille
One-fourth of an inch orange knitting chenille

One-eighth of an inch light gray-green
Two threads orange knitting chenille
Five-eighths of an inch number 4 henna
Two threads orange knitting chenille
Three-sixteenths of an inch number 4 henna
One-half inch light gray-green chenille
Five-eighths of an inch number 3 henna
One-eighth of an inch orange knitting chenille
One-eighth of an inch orange silk
One inch number 5 henna
Three-eighths of an inch orange silk
Three-fourths of an inch number 1 henna
    (This is the center)

Omitting the center, reverse the described pattern for the other half of the weaving. Remove from the loom. (See page 67.) Finish with a two-inch sewed fringe. (See page 69, Plate XXV, Figures A and B.)

## RUGS

The place for the rug determines the material used for its weaving—new materials, of cotton chenille, cotton roving, or cotton cloth, for the bedroom or bathroom in a modern apartment; old materials, for contrast, with colonial or old pine furniture.

### Preparation of Old Materials:

When using old materials sort the cotton, silk, and wool. If old sheets or white cotton are included, put aside some of these to be dyed. Ginghams and materials of similar weight are cut and torn about two and a half inches wide; sateen and light weight cretonne, two inches wide; silkalene or thin muslin, three inches wide; heavy weight cretonne, one and a half inches wide; outing flannel, from one and a half to two inches wide, depending on the weight. Sew together the short lengths (See Plate XXXIII, Figure A) to make a length two yards or more. Wool or silk materials are cut so that, when folded and woven, the rows will be of the same thickness. When all the material is cut and sewed, fold lengthwise, press with a hot iron if necessary, and roll for winding on the blanket shuttles. If new material is used the cotton chenille and the cotton roving comes ready to weave, but cotton cloth must be cut or torn lengthwise; the width depends upon the weight of the cotton.

## RUG FOR THE COTTAGE

The simplicity of design—a few lines of color for a border—allows a wide range for spacing and for colors in this rug.

EQUIPMENT:

>Two-Harness Treadle Loom, 27″, with a 15 dent reed
>Hook for Threading
>3 Blanket Shuttles
>Warp Frame
>Spool Rack

MATERIALS:

>Warp— Carpet warp, ivory colored (6 lbs. will make a ten yard warp or four rugs, each about one and a half yards long.)
>Weft— 10 yds. yellow gingham or chambray
>2 yds. black muslin
>2 yds. orange-yellow sateen
>2 yds. cretonne

*Preparing the Material:*

As it is of rather heavy weight, cut the yellow gingham, (the predominant color), two and one-quarter inches wide. For the border, the black muslin, used as lines of accent, is cut two and three-quarter inches wide; the orange-yellow, two inches wide; the cretonne, two inches wide.

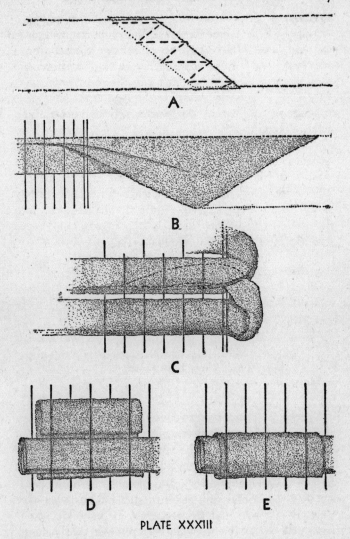

A

B

C

D                    E

PLATE XXXIII

PROCESS:

*Warping:* Warp the loom with four hundred and seven threads, which includes two additional threads for a double thread for each edge. Thread the loom for plain weaving, one thread to each dent of the reed.

*Weaving:* Fold lengthwise, through the center, and wind one strip of the yellow gingham on a shuttle. Leave a four-inch end, and weave two rows. Do not draw in the edges; carry the material around the edge threads in a small one-half inch puff. (See Plate XXXIII, Figure C.) Then open the folded gingham, and cut the end slanting, as shown on Plate XXXIII, Figure B. Tuck the end into the second row. (See Plate XXXIII, Figure C.) Weave five inches of the yellow gingham.

Border
```
1 row of black muslin
2 rows cretonne
1 row black muslin
3 rows yellow gingham
2 rows orange sateen
9 rows cretonne
2 rows orange sateen
3 rows yellow gingham
1 row black muslin
2 rows cretonne
1 row black muslin
```

Weave the center twenty-seven inches long. (Shrinkage will make about a twenty-four inch center when removed from the loom.) Repeat the border. Weave five inches of yellow gingham for the end, drawing in the last four or five rows to match the other end. Weave a one-inch heading of carpet warp. When removing from the loom, leave six inches for a tied fringe. (See Plate XXVII.) Groups of five or six warp ends are suggested as suitable for the knots.

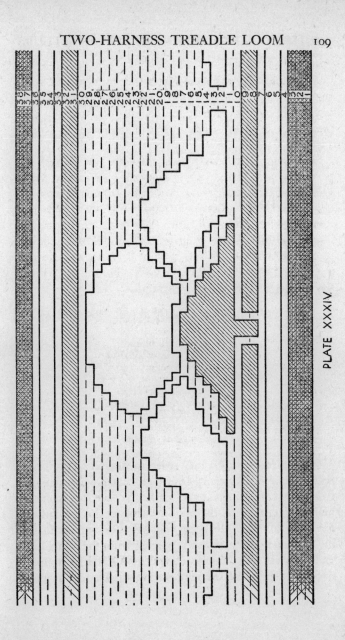

PLATE XXXIV.

## RUG WITH A FLOWERED BORDER

### (*Plate XXXIV*)

This rug, with its conventionalized flower border, is appropriate for the modern tiled bathroom. The flowered effect is formed by wrapping around the rows of background color, contrasting pieces of cloth, cut to given lengths. (See Plate XXXIII, Figures D and E.)

EQUIPMENT:

> Two-Harness Treadle Loom, 36" with a 12 dent reed
> Hook for Threading
> 3 Blanket Shuttles
> Warp Frame
> Spool Rack

MATERIALS:

> Warp— Carpet Warp, gray (7 lbs. makes a 10 yd. warp)
> Weft— 12 yds. blue gingham
> 4 yds. gray gingham
> $1\frac{1}{4}$ yds. dark brown (shown by cross lines on Plate XXXIV)
> 1 yd. gray-green (shown by slanting lines on Plate XXXIV)
> $1\frac{1}{4}$ yds. flowered cretonne
> 1 yd. rose sateen (rows 4 and 5 and 34 and 35 on Plate XXXIV)

(See page 105 for Preparation of Materials.)

PROCESS:

*Warping:* Warp the loom with four hundred and thirty-four threads. This allows for double thread on each edge. Thread the loom for plain weaving with one thread for each dent in the reed.

*Drawing:* Before weaving, it is advisable to draw the figure used in the full sized rug on graph paper (ten squares to an inch) thirty-six inches wide, and about nine inches long. Two squares represent one row of the weaving, and the drawing is translated as follows:

> Three rows dark brown (6 squares represented by crosses on Plate XXXIV)
> One row blue (2 squares)
> Two rows flowered cretonne (4 squares)
> One row gray (2 squares)

*Weaving:*

> One and one-half inch carpet warp for the heading
> Fifteen rows (about 5 inches) blue, the background color of the rug

*Border:*

> Three rows brown (rows 1, 2, and 3 on Plate XXXIV)
> One row blue (row 4 on Plate XXXIV)
> Two rows rose flowered cretonne (rows 5 and 6 on Plate XXXIV)
> One row gray (row 7 on Plate XXXIV)

Use the gray as the background of the flower pattern. All pieces are cut two inches wide, but in varying lengths. For the first three rows of the flower pattern, cut the gray-green in the following lengths:

> Four pieces six and one-fourth inches long
> Nine pieces one-half inch long
> Four pieces ten and three-eighths inches long

Weave one row of gray, battening it to about one-half inch of the last border row of the gray. Measure six and one-half inches from the right edge to the center stem of the first flower, and place a pin as a guide; place another pin eleven and one-fourth inches from that pin (this will be the center of the middle flower, and the middle of the rug); place a third pin eleven and one-quarter inches from the left of the center pin. Fold in, to the center, both edges and one end of the six and one-quarter inch pieces of the gray-green. With the shed for the gray row of the background still open, place this piece of gray-green cloth at the right edge over the gray row. Have the right end of the gray-green just under the double end edge thread with one of the folded edges down over the gray row. Then wrap the upper edge around the back of the gray row. (See Plate XXXIII, Figure D.) Tuck in three of the half-inch lengths in the same way for the flower stems; then two of the ten and three-eighths inch pieces, one each side of the center flower. All four edges of the inside pieces should be folded in so that no rough edge will show in the weaving. When all seven pieces are tucked in, beat the row into place. (Row 8 on Plate XXXIV.) Weave the second row in the same way. (Row 9 on Plate XXXIV.) Weave the third row with a row of background gray, and wrap over it the three remaining pieces of gray-green for the flower stems. (Row 10 on Plate XXXIV.)

Now, the pattern of the flower figure may be followed with the center of each of the three stems for the starting points. The balance of the "laid on" pieces should be cut the following lengths and labeled, by rows, so they will be ready for the weaving.

### Gray-Green Centers for the Flowers

| | | | |
|---|---|---|---|
| 11th row | three pieces | 5¼ | inches |
| 12th " | three pieces | 4⁷⁄₁₆ | " |
| 13th " | three pieces | 3⅜⁄₁₆ | " |
| 14th " | three pieces | 2¾ | " |
| 15th " | three pieces | 2⅜ | " |
| 16th " | three pieces | 1⅝ | " |
| 17th " | three pieces | 1³⁄₁₆ | " |

### Rose Sateen Side Petals for the Flowers

| | | | |
|---|---|---|---|
| 12th row | six pieces | $2\frac{5}{8}$ | inches |
| 13th " | six pieces | $2\frac{13}{16}$ | " |
| 14th " | six pieces | $2\frac{7}{16}$ | " |
| 15th " | six pieces | $2\frac{5}{16}$ | " |
| 16th " | six pieces | $2\frac{13}{16}$ | " |
| 17th " | six pieces | $2\frac{15}{16}$ | " |
| 18th " | six pieces | $2\frac{1}{2}$ | " |
| 19th " | six pieces | $2\frac{5}{16}$ | " |
| 20th " | six pieces | $1\frac{13}{16}$ | " |
| 21st " | six pieces | $1\frac{5}{16}$ | " |
| 22nd " | six pieces | $1\frac{1}{16}$ | " |

### Rose Sateen Center Petals for the Flowers

| | | | |
|---|---|---|---|
| 18th row | six pieces | $\frac{1}{2}$ | inch |
| 19th " | three pieces | $2\frac{5}{8}$ | inches |
| 20th " | three pieces | 3 | " |
| 21st " | three pieces | $3\frac{7}{16}$ | " |
| 22nd " | three pieces | 4 | " |
| 23rd & 24th " | six pieces | $4\frac{1}{4}$ | " |
| 25th " | three pieces | 4 | " |
| 26th " | three pieces | $3\frac{5}{8}$ | " |
| 27th " | three pieces | $3\frac{3}{16}$ | " |
| 28th " | three pieces | $2\frac{13}{16}$ | " |
| 29th " | three pieces | $1\frac{13}{16}$ | " |

## Weave:

One row gray
Two rows brown
One row gray
Two rows flowered cretonne
One row blue
Two rows dark brown (center edge of the border)
Thirty inches of blue (for the center of the rug)
Reverse the border
Fifteen rows of the blue (the end, drawing in the last three
rows to match the other end)

Finish the weaving with one inch of the carpet warp for
the heading. For tying the fringe see page 71, Plate
XXVI.

# GLOSSARY

**APRONS:** 1) The material attached to the warp boom and extending over the whip beam to which the warp is attached.

2) The material attached to the cloth beam and extending over the outside of the breast beam to which the warp is tied, allowing the finished material to be rolled forward.

**BATTEN:** The frame holding the reed.

**BATTENING:** The process of beating the weft threads together.

**BEAMS:** See Cloth Beam, Warp Beam, Roller Beam.

**BEATING:** See Battening.

**BINDER:** This is the weft thread running between the pattern threads to hold them in place.

**BLANKET SHUTTLE:** A wide shuttle for winding a quantity of wool or heavy material.

**BOBBIN SHUTTLE:** The case holds a spool. Used for carrying the weft thread in the weaving, and thrown through the shed from one hand to the other.

**BORDER:** A decoration along the end or the margin of any article.

**BORDER, CONVENTIONALIZED:** Balancing or bringing into harmony the parts of a flower, as a unit of pattern.

**BREAST BEAM:** The front beam of a loom over which the cloth passes.

**CLOTH BEAM:** The front roller beam on which the finished material is wound.

**CROSS:** The crossing of threads in winding the warp.

**DENT:** The space between the vertical bars of the reed through which the warp is threaded.

**DOG AND RATCHET:** See Ratchet and Wheel.

**DRAFT:** The pattern drawn on squared or cross-sectioned paper to show the correct threading for its design.

**DRAUGHT:** Draft.

**DRAWING IN:** Threading warp ends through the heddles or reed.

**ENTERING HOOK:** See Threading Hook.

EYE: Center space in the heddle.

FILLING: The commercial term for weft.

FLY SHUTTLE: The shuttle thrown through the shed on the shuttle race by pulling a stick or cord.

FRAME: See Warp Frame.

GROOVED SHUTTLE: Has pointed ends and grooved sides, into which fits the winding of the yarn.

HARNESS: Frame holding heddles.

HEADLE: Heddle.

HEALDS: Heddles.

HEDDLES: Cords or wires each containing an eye to hold a warp thread.

HEDDLE FRAME: Harness.

HOOK: See Threading Hook.

HORSES: Wooden pieces formerly used on old looms. These were suspended from the upper horizontal frame of loom by pulleys and attached at either end by cords extending to the harnesses.

LEASE: See Cross.

LEASE PEGS: Pegs on a warp frame between which the cross is made.

LEASE STICKS: Sticks inserted in each shed, with the cross or lease between.

LAMBS: The horizontal levers extending between the harnesses and treadles to which they are connected by cords or chains for the raising or lowering of the harness.

LATHE or SLEY: Originally applied to a stick used to batten the weft threads in weaving. Term now applied to reed and frame.

LOOM: Frame of any kind on which warp may be fastened for weaving.

LOOM FRAME: The framework for supporting or holding the working parts of the loom.

NEEDLES:

  2"—A large needle with a blunt point for fastening the ends of threads.

  6"—A straight needle with blunt point for weaving on small frames.

  5"—A needle with a curved point for weaving on large frames.

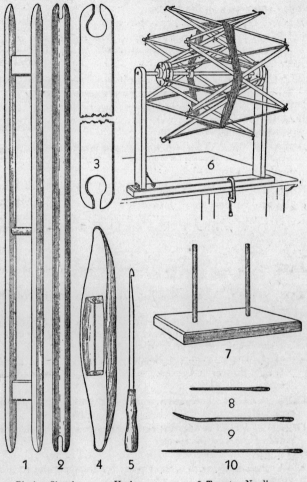

1 Blanket Shuttle
2 Grooved Shuttle
3 Flat Stick Shuttle
4 Bobbin Shuttle

5 Hook
6 Swift
7 Spool Rack

8 Tapestry Needle
9 Curved 5" Needle
10 Blunt pointed 6" Needle

PICK: A row of weft.

PICKING: The movement of a weft thread through the shed.

PLY: Denotes the number of strands, closely wound together; two ply two strands, four ply four strands.

RACE: The front block in a batten on which the fly shuttle runs.

RADDLE: A device for spreading the warp threads evenly as they are wound on the warp beam. Not in common use.

RATCHET AND WHEEL: A catch fitted into the teeth of a wheel on the ends of either a warp or a cloth beam to control the winding action of the beam.

REPEAT OF THE PATTERN: Used in weaving to describe a unit which may be repeated a number of times in either the warp or the weft threads.

REED: The comb-like part of the batten that holds the warp threads an equal distance apart and beats the weft threads into place.

ROD HEDDLE: A cord around a rod, in front of the shed rod and used to open the second shed.

ROLLER BEAM: The beam for changing the sheds on the Two-Harness Table Loom.

SELVAGE: The side edges of the finished weaving or web.

SHED: Opening in warp thread through which the shuttle or weft is passed.

SHED ROD: A flat stick run over and under alternate warp threads, and turned on edge as the weft is passed through.

SKEIN: Loosely coiled length of thread or yarn.

SLEY: See Batten, Lathe, and Reed.

SPOOL RACK: Device for holding two spools.

SPREADER: See Raddle.

STICK BATTEN: The shed rod turned flat and struck against each weft thread as it is put in.

STICK SHUTTLE: A flat stick with the weft wound on it lengthwise.

SWIFT: An adjustable rack for holding a skein of yarn.

TABBY: Plain weaving.

TEMPLE: An implement for keeping the web stretched an even width while weaving.

TENSION: The stretch of the threads used for the warp while in the loom.

TIE-UP: The process of tying the lambs to the treadles.

THREADING HOOK: A thin hook used for drawing in or entering threads through the heddles or the reed.

TREADLE: The pedal-like part of the loom operated by the feet.

TUBE: The spool on which the thread is wound.

TWO-BAR LOOM: Two non-revolving bars over which the warp is passed.

WARP: The threads running lengthwise on the loom.

WARPING: Preparing and putting warp on the loom.

WARPING BARS: or WARPING FRAME: The wooden frame with pegs for making small warps.

WARP BEAM: Roll at back of loom on which the warp is wound.

WARP CHAIN: A chain made of the warp in removing it from the warp frame.

WARP FRAME: See Warping Bars.

WARPING DRUM or MILL: Cylindrical frame on which the long warps are made.

WEAVES: Plain Weave or Tabby Weave has every other thread in the warp picked up, first by one shed, and then by the other.
  Basket Weave: Two threads or more, used together, both in the warp and the weft.
  Alternate Weave: Two threads and a single thread used in alternation, either in the warp or the weft, or in both.

WEB: The finished woven material.

WEFT: The threads that cross the warp.

WINDING PIN: Tool used for turning warp or cloth beam.

WHEEL: See Ratchet.

WHIP BEAM: Beam at the back of the loom over which the warp passes.

WOOF: Weft.

YARN: A thread of any kind.

# MATERIALS

## COTTONS FOR WARPS

The least expensive cotton 20/2 is the fine, and is generally used. This is a good cotton with linen, as it has a soft finish without gloss.

EGYPTIAN: A stronger cotton with more twist to it, sizes 24/3–16/3–16/4.

MERCERIZED COTTON: Having a gloss or shine, it combines well with silk and coarser mercerized cottons.

MERCERIZED PEARL COTTON: Pearl No. 3, the coarser, is used for runners, heavy bags, embroidery weaves, and pattern weaving for Indian designs.

> Pearl No. 5, slightly finer. Used for weft, also as warp, for heavy curtains and couch covers.

> Pearl No. 10 and No. 20 for the warp and binder or tabby in pattern weaving.

> Perleen, the mercerized strand cotton, for—runners, bags of all kinds, the front pieces of house sandals, and chair backs.

CARPET WARP: A large size dull-finished cotton. Carpet warp, as a weft with a mercerized No. 10 for warp, is most effective in its gay colors for table covers, porch pillows, and chair seats for the country house.

## COTTON FOR WEFT OR FILLER

UMBRIAN: A colored cotton, size 20/2, also used as a warp if desired.

PERUGIAN FILLER: Size 12/2, a colored cotton good as a fine filler.

VITTORA STRAND: A dull-finished strand cotton similar to that used in much of the Italian weaving.

## WEFT FOR RUGS

BERNAT'S RUGRO: 4-ply, soft, loose twist cotton heavy enough so that the rug will lie flat.

COTTON CHENILLE: A fluffy cut cotton suitable for face cloths, bath mats, and rugs. It comes in light pastel colors.

COTTON ROVING: A 4-ply cotton for rugs.

## LINEN

WARP: For this a twisted 2-ply or 3-ply linen only should be used. This comes in 10/2 white, and natural,—40/3 and 40/2 both white and natural; 40/2 may be had in colors.

WEFTS: The above warps may be used, or the soft and loosely twisted flax thread in Tow Bleach 14 and 20, Tow Natural 10, 14, and 20, superfine white in 10, 14, 20, and 25, also colored linens in fine, medium, and linen floss.

RAYON: This is a weft that is very glossy and gives an almost metallic effect. Used for pattern weaving.

BOUCLIN: This may be used effectively for bags and runners.

TINSEL: Silver, gilt, bronze, and copper threads are effective as binder or tabby in pattern weaving.

## SILK

SPUN SILK: Made of silk waste. The finest grades are twisted and doubled making a soft, strong warp. The coarser may be used for the weft.

SPUN SILK FLOSS: A coarse type.

STRAND SILK: Like strand cotton has many slightly spun strands loosely twisted together. Used for bags, purses, and scarfs, when a heavier quality of silk is needed.

TWISTED SILK: This must be used for the warp.

WILD SILK: One of the best silks for weaving as its unevenness gives an interesting texture to the fabric, and is effective in pattern weaving for underarm purses, change purses or other small articles. The name Wild Silk comes from the fact that the worms are hatched in the open, rather than in nurseries. This is also true of the Tussah silks from India and China.

## WOOL

A wide variety of wool, and wool and rayon yarns have come into the market within the last few years because of the revival of knitting.

For tapestry weaving of a simple type, the widest range of colors is in the heavy Tapestry wools. The English Crewel wool may be used where the light weight wools are practical.

The cheapest substitute for Tapestry wool is Peasant wool which comes in a good range of colors.

Ranging down in price between Tapestry wool and Peasant wool comes first, the heaviest knitting worsted, then Germantown worsted, and Shetland Floss.

The Shetland Floss has the widest range of uses being fine enough for wool neck scarfs, and yet coarse enough for the making of tapestry bags, etc.

Laurel, a rayon worsted mixture in pastel colors, is useful in combination with Shetland Floss.

Fabri and Afghan, being soft and strong, make satisfactory wools for firmly woven neck scarfs, or light weight dress material.

Homespun may be used for both warp and weft when a rougher texture is desired for bags, chair coverings, and rugs.

Angora, made of rabbit's wool, is very soft and fluffy, often used for sweaters, etc.

Miro, a yarn of special twist rayon and worsted, is soft and colorful; used for neck scarfs.

## NEWER YARNS

BOUCLÉ: A rough textured rayon.

BOUCLÉ DE LAINE: Similar to bouclé, but of a much softer texture.

CASHMERE YARN: Cashmere and worsted, soft and good for neck scarfs.

SPANISH STOCKING YARN: A yarn in neutral colors, combining well with strand of brilliant color; used in scarfs, neckties, and light weight blankets.

YORKSHIRE: Australian worsted comes in a wide range of delightful colors, useful for weaving material for hats, scarfs, bags, and other articles to match dresses and coats.

RUG WOOL: Obtainable in fine or medium weights and a variety of colors.

SMYRNA RUG WORSTED: A lustrous rug yarn obtainable in soft colors. A few bright colors may be used for accents.